You bet your tomatoes!

Fun Facts, Tall Tales, and a Handful of Useful Gardening Tips

MIKE McGRATH

D0557173

RODALE

RODALE

WE **INSPIRE** AND **ENABLE** PEOPLE TO IMPROVE
THEIR LIVES AND THE WORLD AROUND THEM

Editor: Deborah L. Martin
Interior Book Designer: John Pepper
Cover Designer: Gavin Robinson
Interior and Cover Illustrator: Signe Wilkinson
Layout Designer: Keith Biery
Researcher: Diana Erney
Copy Editor: Sarah Sacks Dunn
Product Specialist: Jodi Schaffer
Indexer: Nan Badgett

Rodale Organic Living Books

Editorial Director: Christopher Hirsheimer
Executive Creative Director: Christin Gangi
Executive Editor: Kathleen DeVanna Fish
Art Director: Patricia Field
Content Assembly Manager: Robert V. Anderson Jr.
Studio Manager: Leslie M. Keefe
Copy Manager: Nancy N. Bailey
Projects Coordinator: Kerrie A. Cadden

We're always happy to hear from you. For questions or comments concerning the editorial content of this book, please write to:
Rodale Book Readers' Service
33 East Minor Street
Emmaus, PA 18098
Look for other Rodale books wherever books are sold. Or call us at (800) 848-4735.
For more information about Rodale Organic Living books and magazines, visit us at
www.organicgardening.com

Library of Congress Cataloging-in-Publication Data

McGrath, Mike.
   You bet your tomatoes! : fun facts, tall tales, and a handful of useful garden tips / Mike McGrath.
       p.   cm.
    ISBN 0–87596–870–8 (pbk. : alk. paper)
    1. Tomatoes.   2. Tomatoes—Humor.   I. Title.
 SB349 .M38 2002
 635'.642'0207—dc21   2001005502

Distributed in the book trade by St. Martin's Press
2 4 6 8 10 9 7 5 3 1   paperback

Rodale

Organic Gardening Starts Here!

Here at Rodale, we've been gardening organically for more than 60 years—ever since my grandfather J. I. Rodale learned about composting and decided that healthy living starts with healthy soil. In 1940 J. I. started the Rodale Organic Farm to test his theories, and today the nonprofit Rodale Institute Experimental Farm is still at the forefront of organic gardening and farming research. In 1942 J. I. founded *Organic Gardening* magazine to share his discoveries with gardeners everywhere. His son, my father, Robert Rodale, headed *Organic Gardening* until 1990, and today a third generation of Rodales is growing up with the new *OG*. Over the years we've shown millions of readers how to grow bountiful crops and beautiful flowers using nature's own techniques.

In this book, you'll find the latest organic methods and the best gardening advice. We know—because all our authors and editors are passionate about gardening! We feel strongly that our gardens should be safe for our children, pets, and the birds and butterflies that add beauty and delight to our lives and landscapes. Our gardens should provide us with fresh, flavorful vegetables, delightful herbs, and gorgeous flowers. And they should be a pleasure to work in as well as to view.

Sharing the secrets of safe, successful gardening is why we publish books. So come visit us at www.organicgardening.com, where you can tour the world of gardening all day, every day. And use this book to create your best garden ever.

Happy gardening!

Maria Rodale

Maria Rodale
Rodale Organic Gardening Books

For J. I. and Bob Rodale, who carved it all out of solid rock.

History buffs take note: Bob Rodale told his readers about a
new book called *Silent Spring* in the 20th anniversary issue of
Organic Gardening (*and Farming* back then)!

I'm extremely proud to have been a small part of this
grand tradition, which has been saving the planet one farm
and garden at a time since 1942. **Organic forever!**
—Mike McGrath, 2001*

(*Aren't we supposed to be uncovering monoliths on the moon by now?)

CONTENTS

WHY AM I DOING **THIS** INSTEAD OF ENJOYING MY SUMMER???

Sooner or later, all those people who claim to be gardeners *(or Italian)* have to grow their own fresh, vine-ripened summer tomatoes. *(Unless they live in Arizona, southern California, Texas, Florida, or some other godforsaken place so hot they have to grow tomatoes over the winter and then live in deep holes in the sand all summer to escape the heat, like toads and people who make up cellular-phone calling plans.)*

Resistance is futile. So you might as well accept the inevitable and start staggering around the garden getting your tomatoes in nice and early this season—that way you **MIGHT** end up with some actual **ripe** ones before Hard Frost comes a-knocking.

Yes, the simple truth is, like other things you have no interest in doing *(and/or live in abject fear of)*, like climbing that big mountain or buying a minivan, if you claim the gardening mantle, you must grow tomatoes "because they are there." Well, actually they **aren't** there yet. But they sure **will** be once you get growing, won't they?! Yeah. Right.

Anyway, there are lots of neat **actual** reasons why you should grow your own tomatoes. Here are just a few:

■ All of the tomatoes for sale in grocery stores are now genetically engineered, with most varieties containing DNA taken from Regis Philbin, Alex Trebek, Wink Martindale, Whoopi Goldberg, Pat Sajak, or some other game-show type when they weren't paying attention.

- You can't quite afford a boat but still have a desperate need to show your neighbors that you know how to foolishly waste your time and money in a really pointless manner.
- They're easier to grow than watermelons...
- ... and it's **LOTS** easier to tell when they're ripe.
- Most other summertime endeavors have a much higher risk of death and/or dismemberment.
- You'll have a handy excuse for avoiding those treacherous family reunion picnics, mosquito- and blackfly-infested hikes, frolics in freezing cold ocean waves, and other festive seasonal outings you'd be dragged to if you couldn't say, **"Gee, I'd love to,** but I performed a special 'biodynamic copper flange pruning technique' on my tomato plants last night, and I have to stay here and spray them with compost tea every hour until Tuesday or the pistils won't be firm."
- You'll be able to throw around gardening terms like "pistil" and "compost tea" without being laughed at. Maybe.
- There's probably something even more tedious that you'd have to do **inside** the house if you didn't have the tomatoes to herd.
- You'll have a great reason *(OK—"excuse," but it's your word against theirs)* to buy, rent, or borrow a big tiller and thus use a really noisy, dangerous piece of gasoline-powered equipment!
- You can wait until those annoying neighbors *(oh, come on—you know **EXACTLY** who I mean)* have company over in their oh-so-perfect backyard to fire up that really noisy piece of power equipment.
- You'll be able to cut the family food bill by a good $30 or $40 a year—while spending less than the cost of a new car to grow your own tomatoes!

- When your kids complain that they're bored for the 368th time that summer *(and school's only been out for a month)*, you can say, "Well, you could always weed the tomatoes."
- You can say it **A LOT.**

REASON #562

But seriously, folks, there is one **BIG,** overwhelming reason you really **SHOULD** grow your own tomatoes:

1. There is honestly nothing that can compare to the taste of a fresh, vine-ripened tomato, plucked at the perfect peak of sweetness and eaten warm and sugary and tart and juicy right there in the garden as you make a big mess all over your shirt.

2. If you actually get good at this *(and you can—I grow GREAT tomatoes just about every season and I barely have opposable thumbs)*, you'll have access to the ultimate summertime bragging right: "Oh, and would you like a slice of fresh tomato on that? Let me go out and pick a nice one for you." **YYYEEESSSSSS!!!!**

3. If you get **REALLY** good at it, you can go for the gold: Having ripe, red tomatoes **OBVIOUSLY** hanging on your plants **DAYS** before that pain-in-the-butt gardener down the block who's been showing off for **YEARS.**

4. And then nirvana: Knocking on that P-I-T-B gardener's door in late June with a bag of ripe tomatoes and saying, "Here—I noticed that your plants don't seem to be doing very well this year, and we've had more than we can eat for weeks now."

5. Start your own tomatoes from **seed** *(get back here—gardening isn't for the timid! And death, after all, is inevitable! Part of the great circle of life! It'll be like you're in a Disney movie!)*, and you can grow *(and share and savor and* **REALLY** *brag about)* wonderful varieties that you just can't find already started for you at the garden center, much less in the supermarket, like *Tigerella, Brandywine, Big Rainbow, Radiator Charlie's Mortgage Lifter. . . .*

Well, yes, that **IS** actually five reasons, and yes, I **DID** begin by writing that "there is one big overwhelming reason you should grow your own. . . ." There is/are a/an excellent explanation(s) for this:

■ What are you—a cop?
■ There is only one. *You* have to figure out **WHICH** one it is. *(But don't worry; you still have all your lifelines intact.)*
■ I thought you should know early on here that you're about to take gardening advice from a man who can't count. To 1.
■ Hey, you already bought the book—what do I care? *("Another bottle of Dom Perignon, garçon—and a side of fries!")*

Alright—enough philosophy. It's time to get our hands dirty and start killing some tomatoes! . . . er, **planting** some tomatoes. That's what I actually **meant** to say: **planting.** *(It's not my fault; I have a cold.)*

CHAPTER 1

"Picking" Your Tomatoes

(Do all of these things have funny, rude, or mysterious names?)

Well, no—but those other ones aren't worth growing. Anyway, tomatoes are like wine—because all the good ones are red! *(White wine is something you drink when you're sick, like tea.)* Actually, **un**like wine, some of the best tomatoes aren't red *(but they ain't white either, tea drinkers!)*.

But really I say that tomatoes **are** like wine because you often have the most fun when you break the "rules." There are no "wrong" tomatoes; you should grow what you like.

So I'll provide a few basic facts and distinctions—like how big the various plants and fruits will get and how long you'll have to wait to get ripe tomatoes. But beyond that, I want you to fall in love with weird names and romantic illusions and grow as many different flights of fancy as you can. Some will become your tomatoes forever, while others will prove to be nothing more than a one-season stand. That's okay—you're young and foolish, and we don't judge. *(Unless you dismiss the flavor of a first-rate tomato like big juicy* Brandywine *as "mealy" or something, and then you're just* **hopeless!** *Other than* **that,** *we don't judge.)*

WHAT'S YOUR TOMATO DETERMINATION?

Sometimes this "there are two types of . . . " thing gets out of hand. *(My favorite is, "There are two types of people—those who break society down into two types of people, and those who don't," which I attribute to Oscar Wilde but might have read in a comic book.)* But with tomatoes—there really **are** two main types of plants, and the difference is important.

Determinate plants tend to pretty much stop growing around the time their tomatoes form, produce all of their fruits in one big flush, and are then mostly done for the season. Obviously such plants are great for large-scale farming, but they're also good for gardeners *(like moi)* who cook down most of their crop to jar up for the winter: You can pick, cook, and be done. That's probably why most—but not all—paste tomatoes are determinate. The plants also tend to be smaller and more compact, making them good choices for small-space and container gardens. **AND** you can pull up those plants when they're done in mid- to late summer and replace them with nice big batches of lettuce, spinach, broccoli, and/or other fall crops!

Indeterminate plants grow like big honking pumpkins. Their vines don't stop creeping toward the next county until they're killed by frost *(although they'll slow down quite a bit when the days get shorter and the nights get cooler)*. They produce flowers and fruits throughout the season, making them great choices for folks who simply like to enjoy a nice steady supply of fresh tomatoes all summer long. The plants tend to be sprawling and quite the opposite of compact. Most of the old, great-tasting heirloom varieties— and big tomatoes in general—are indeterminate. **Note:** The yield on such plants is often smaller than that of the more compact varieties, **but**

■ sometimes their extended tomato production time evens things out, and

■ the bigger, better-tasting heirloom tomatoes need a larger "leaf-to-fruit ratio" to create those big, complex flavors. As a result, their fewer fruits have much richer flavor. As with wine grapes *(what is it with this guy? Will somebody just get him a drink?!)*, the smaller the harvest, the more intense the flavor of the fruits.

MORE STUFF TO THINK ABOUT

Once you've determined whether you want your tomatoes to be determinate or indeterminate, you'll probably want to lie down and rest for awhile. Well, too bad! Tomato growing isn't for wimps. There are still a bunch of other seed catalog variables you'll want to consider in making your choice.

DAYS TO MATURITY (DTM)

You should see this info—a certain number of days—listed for every variety in seed catalogs and, if you're lucky, on those little "ID stakes" in nursery

6-packs. This is **supposed** to define the average number of days it will take before you bite into your first ripe tomato but is instead, like many things in life and gardening, a damned lie. It is **actually** the number of days it will take the average **6-week-old transplant** to produce edible fruit. So for plants you start from seed, add 50 days to that number *(the extra week is for the seeds to germinate)*. *(And since these numbers are mostly found on* **seed** *packets, why should we have to do the math?)* Still, DTMs are very useful numbers for comparison, **especially** if you live in a frozen latitude. A short growing season means you should stick with tomatoes with the lowest DTMs, even if you intend to start 'em early, protect 'em with special warming things like Wallo'Waters early in the season, and so forth. And yes, if you have a looonnnggg season, **do** look for big numbers. Take advantage of what some others of us **don't** have—lots of growing days—and enjoy the rarest and best-tasting heirlooms, some of which can take what seems like **forever** to produce fruit.

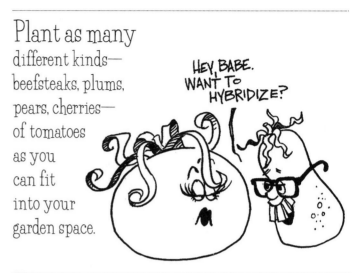

Plant as many different kinds—beefsteaks, plums, pears, cherries—of tomatoes as you can fit into your garden space.

HEY, BABE. WANT TO HYBRIDIZE?

TYPE

You got your huge beefsteaks, your pasters, your sweet, invasive little cherries *(a.k.a. weeds)*, and your regular round tomatoes. If you got the room, grow at least one of each type. Most of the beefsteak types are also great for processing, and they add a lot of distinctive tomato flavor to the finished sauce. And many folks rave about slicing pasters up for use as sandwich tomatoes—no messy juice!

However, DON'T grow cherry tomatoes unless you

    A) have **LOTS** of room *(they can make pumpkin vines look indecisive)*;

    B) grow for fresh eating *(how many cherry tomatoes would it take to make a pint of sauce???)*;

    C) don't mind bazillions of volunteer cherry tomato plants coming up in your garden for decades to come; and

    D) have LOTS of room. *(Or you can choose one of the determinate types of cherry tomatoes—they're not such terrible space hogs.)*

OPEN-POLLINATED OR HYBRID

Science time, class! Oh, get back here—it's not that bad. Essentially, the difference is that if you save seeds from the fruit of an **open-pollinated** variety such as *Brandywine* and plant them the following year, you will grow the same type of plant with the same kind of fruit.

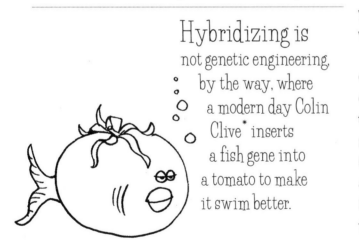

Hybridizing is not genetic engineering, by the way, where a modern day Colin Clive* inserts a fish gene into a tomato to make it swim better.

Hybrids are the product of a deliberate mating of two different varieties in order to combine two desirable characteristics—like, for instance, to get some improved disease resistance into a very tasty but disease-prone type. The process of creating hybrid seed is fairly complex and very labor-intensive. Basically, you force two different *(but consenting)* plants to have sex with each other, then protect those flowers and fruits from outside interference *(usually by covering them with paper bags)*, and then harvest seeds that, when grown, will produce something

*Colin Clive played Dr. Frankenstein *("It's alive! Alive! Hahahaha!")* in the original Boris Karloff movies.

different from either of the parents—like those bratty kids of yours. If you grow a hybrid tomato, save the seeds, and then plant them the following season, you will not get the same plants or fruits. You will get tomato plants, but they might not be very good ones.

BY LAW, HYBRID PLANTS AND SEEDS MUST BE IDENTIFIED BY THE WORD **"HYBRID"** OR THE TERM **"F1."**

Some hard-line organic folks oppose hybrids on the grounds that they're not "natural" plants, but there's nothing diabolical—or even bad—about the process, and once again, it has nothing to do with gene-jerking around. For the record, I don't mind hybrid varieties, and some folks really need 'em. Most of the varieties that have been **proven** to be resistant to specific diseases and pests are hybrids, for instance. So go ahead and grow a few if you like—just don't save the seeds to start next year's crop.

Now let's move on to some of your best choices. Organized, because I said so, by type *(beefsteak, paste, etc.)*.

I AM
AN HEIRLOOM!

OH, WAIT A MINUTE: HEIRLOOMS!

"Heirloom" tomatoes are at the root *(get it, "root"? arf! arf! Gee, I just break myself up . . .)* of tomato gardening. Some were **never** available commercially in "the old days"; others **were** available but were discontinued decades ago. But the people who kept these gems alive **really** liked these varieties and saved some seeds from their best tomatoes season after season so they could continue to grow them, often because they were unique in some way: flavor, color *(some wild ones!)*, durability, size, disease resistance, productivity, etc. By definition, therefore, all heirlooms are open-pollinated varieties. Thanks to a renaissance in **true tomato** interest, the seeds of many of these great varieties are once again available to all.

TOP TOMATOES

Variety Name	Determinate (D) or Indeterminate (I)	Hybrid (H) or Open-Pollinated (OP)	Days to Maturity
Beefsteaks and Slicers			
Arkansas Traveler*	I	OP	89
Big Beef†	I	H	73
Big Boy	I	OP	78
Better Boy†	I	H	70
Big Rainbow*	I	OP	100
Black Krim	I	OP	85
Brandywine	I	OP	80
Celebrity†	D	H	70
Cherokee Purple	I	OP	80
Early Girl†	I	H	52
Georgia Streak	I	OP	90
German Johnson*	I	OP	76
Lemon Boy	I	OP	75
Mortgage Lifter	I	OP	79
Oregon Spring†	D	OP	60
Park's Whopper Improved†	I	H	65
Rutgers†	D	OP	75
Stupice†	I	OP	60
Tigerella (a.k.a. Mr. Stripey)	I	OP	60

*Heirloom variety that, over time, has shown itself to be disease- and/or pest-resistant

†Proven to be resistant to specific diseases and/or pests

Comments

Legendary pink heirloom; can handle hot and dry climates; good in South

Best producer of the really huge tomatoes; old-time tomato flavor

Thick-walled, meaty 1-pounder

Want **TONS** of tomatoes? One plant can produce hundreds of pounds!

Huge, beautiful, tasty heirloom; red streaks on gold; takes heat well

DELICIOUS, productive, dependable, cold-tolerant, dark purple Russian heirloom

Huge heirloom! Quite possibly best-tasting tomato; pink, red, and yellow types

Medium-large fruits; often flawless appearance; hugely dependable; tasty, too!

A tomato grown by Native Americans! Purple-pink, delicious, super-productive heirloom

Super-dependable, **EARLY,** productive, tasty, medium-size slicers; a classic!

The prettiest I ever grew; yellow with red streaks; big and flavorful!

A classic pinkish red heirloom; more productive and faster to produce than most

Light yellow color; tasty, meaty fruits; a heavy producer

The biggest fruits you can grow, sez me; delicious, pinkish red 2- to 3-pounders

Very productive and extremely cold-tolerant; a short-season winner!

Previously OG50; big tasty tomatoes; thrives under poor conditions; early

A true classic all-around tomato; pretty, productive, and very juicy

Remarkable heirloom; **VERY** flavorful cold-tolerant variety; productive and early, too

A little red tomato with yellow-orange stripes; tangy, productive, and early

(continued)

TOP TOMATOES—CONTINUED

Variety Name	Determinate (D) or Indeterminate (I)	Hybrid (H) or Open-Pollinated (OP)	Days to Maturity
Pasters			
Amish Paste	I	OP	82
Bellstar	D	OP	72
Opalka	I	OP	75
Roma†	D	OP	75
San Marzano	I	OP	80
Cherries			
Green Grape	D	OP	75
Riesentraube	I	OP	76
Sun Gold	I	H	57
Supersweet 100	I	H	63
Sweet Chelsea†	I	H	66
Sweet Million†	I	H	65
Sweet 100	I	H	65
Tumbler	D	H	49
Yellow Pear	I	OP	80

†Proven to be resistant to specific diseases and/or pests

Comments

Huge fruits; tasty, productive, flavorful heirloom; great all-purpose tomato

A personal fave; large, productive heirloom; great taste fresh and in sauce

Large, sweet, banana-shaped fruits; **VERY** meaty Polish heirloom

Great taste; extraordinarily productive and dependable; **THE** classic paster

Drop-dead gorgeous fruits; **very** tasty; super-reliable, too

Green when ripe but tastes great; a fun grow! Amaze your friends!

Translation: "Giant bunch of grapes;" flavorful heirloom grows in clusters

Early yellow-orange sweetie; unique mild tropical citrusy flavor

Just as flavorful as the original, with improved disease resistance; early

Large (for a cherry) and super disease- and pest-resistant

Another improvement! Early and hugely productive with larger fruits

The original "never-ending vine" extra-sweet cherry; the standard

For those with no space; tasty fruits on **VERY** compact plants; very early

Golden-colored, pear-shaped, super-sweet–flavored heirloom; hugely productive

the Joy of Germination

(Or, Killing Your Own Tomatoes from Seed)

Now that you've selected the tomato varieties you intend to terrorize over the next several months, it's time to turn those tiny little seeds into gigantic plants bursting with luscious ripe fruit!

Get back here! You can do this! Starting tomatoes isn't really difficult, like growing eggplant or watermelons! *(On the other hand, it ain't zucchini either.)* Tomatoes are one of the easiest plants you can start yourself! Provided you don't screw up this part, that is.

First, some math! To figure out when to start your seeds, you need to have some idea of when you hope to put actual living plants out into the garden. Put those plants out too early and the poor little babies will freeze to death. Do it too late and you won't get as many tomatoes as you could have, unless you live in Syracuse, and then you won't get any.

First, find out what the average last-frost date is for your area. Ever since *USA Today* took over the world of journalism, God help us if six pages goes by without a chart. So just imagine that there's a chart here. If you're compulsive about such things, call your local Cooperative Extension office *(look in the blue pages of your phone book)* and ask 'em what your average last-frost date is. They **live** for this kind of stuff. Otherwise, don't worry: If you live on the East Coast or in the Midwest at or above the Carolinas, you can safely put your plants out around the 1st of June and pretty much count on success. If you live in one of them fancy areas *(like where it never frosts)*, well, it doesn't really much matter when you put **yours** out, now does it? **They're not going to FREEZE, are they??? Pbbblllfffffytttt!!!!** *(Sorry—I had to shovel a lot of snow last year. WET snow.)*

Now some books would provide a big ol' hairy chart here that reveals frost dates. But the truth is that even the finest, most excellently configured such charts usually look like somebody used the book to swat a fly and caught it right about where your garden should be.

Anyway, you want to allow your seeds a week or so *(call it 10 days to be safe—especially with you)* to germinate and a **FULL** 6 weeks *(they're still going to look pretty puny at that age, so no cheating!)* to grow some before you consider putting them out into the cold, cruel world, which you should do only "after all chance of frost is gone."

You know what that last part means, don't you? Right—**you** will now have the power to cause the latest frost in the history of your region! It's easy! Just call up your local TV weather guesser and say, "I'm going to make it frost on Thursday!"

"How are you going to do that? It's supposed to be mild—50s at night and 60 during the day."

"I'm putting my tomatoes out on Wednesday."

"Wait a minute—hold on! . . . Sorry—what did you say? I got distracted for a second—a huge cold front just came heaving down out of Canada on the radar all of a sudden!"

timing your tomatoes

OK, now let's say you're like me and you plan to plant on June 1, a date that has always served me well. Here's the math:

10 days for germination	10
6 weeks to grow some	+45 *(my weeks are longer than yours)*
1 week to harden-off	+10 *(I like round numbers, what can I say? And yes, we'll explain what "hardening off" means later—keep your pants on!)*
Total	=65 days

So round off all the extras I added, and let's call it 2 months. That means you could safely start your seeds anywhere between mid-March and April 1.

Why as early as mid-March? **1)** It won't hurt a bit if the plants are a little older *(and bigger)* when they go out. And **2)** what if you screw up and your first run of starts all die? Honor dictates that you try again at least once before you go and buy the strange-looking overfed *Big Boys* at Wal-Mart! *(Besides, there are a lot of seeds in those packets . . .)*

But you **won't** fail, and they **won't** die! *(Unless, like I said, you screw up . . .)*

Where I live in Pennsylvania, the average last-frost date is May 15. Many people have been confused by that terminology into thinking that this means it won't ever frost on the 16th of May. Uh-uh. **"On average"** it won't. And you can imagine how much your poor plants will care about odds and averages when they're looking for scrap wood to burn in little barrels as they rapidly lose the feeling in their little branches, and stuff that looks suspiciously like snow begins to mulch them.

So my advice is for you to plan to put your sweet, trusting little plants in the garden about 2 weeks **after** that average last-frost date. Don't forget that tomatoes are tropical plants, and unless you go to lots of trouble to keep them warm, they'll just sit out there being resentful until the nights warm up into reliable mid-50s.

TOMATO-STARTING STUFF

One of the great things about gardening is that it almost always means that you get to go out and buy lots of stuff and actually claim you're going to save money by doing so. It's probably going to turn out to be a damned lie, but hey—the shopping is still fun. Here's what you need to get your tomato babies growing:

- Tomato seeds *(d'uh!)*

- The plastic 6-packs that last year's tomato *(or marigold or impatiens or . . .)* plants came in. *(Don't have any handy? Well, bum some from another gardener—I got* **HUNDREDS!***)* Don't use folklore stuff like cutoff milk cartons or egg cartons. You need something made of plastic that drains well and is about the size of . . . well, the size of nursery plant 6-packs!

23

■ Seed-starting mix. **NOT** your lousy garden soil! Listen to me now and this becomes the first time I save your life *(well, actually the life of your tomatoes-to-be, but I love drama)*! It probably won't be the last, but your tender charges **will** be dead if you ignore my warning!

■ Something to sit the 6-packs in that will hold them and water, like an old baking dish *(or dishes)* or one of them big aluminum *(check for pinholes in the bottom first!)* trays that the caterer left behind. Or even—call me crazy—one of those plastic flats *(the sans-hole kind)* that actual plant professionals use for holding plastic 6-packs of seedlings.

■ A fluorescent shop light with two 4-foot-long 40-watt tubes. No, your "sunny windowsill" is NOT good enough. *(Did you know that "sunny windowsill" is actually Latin for "that's why your plants died"?)*. And 25-watt tubes ain't good enough either. Although a **FOUR**-tube light fixture **is** way better! You be the man with a four-tuber, baby!

■ Something to eventually feed the young plants with, like a little finished compost or a nice gentle organic fertilizer, like a seaweed/fish mixture.

OK, everything assembled? Good. Now mix all the ingredients together, cover with aluminum foil, and bake in a 350°F oven for 40 minutes, then . . . oh, no . . . wait a minute—that's the fish recipe for tonight's dinner. Never mind.

READY, SET, START!

About that seed-starting mixture: One of the secrets of your impending success will be the fact that you wisely chose **NOT** to use your lousy garden soil (LGS) to start your seeds. That's because you **know** your LGS will turn into concrete and kill the poor things faster than even you could have. No, these little sprouties need a nice loose "mix" that both retains moisture **and** drains well. Impossible, you say? Nay, say I!

The ideal way to achieve this is to buy a bag of perlite, which looks like little Styrofoam balls but is actually an incredibly lightweight, mined, "popped" mineral, and a bag of vermiculite, which looks like little pieces off the back of a broken mirror but is also light-of-weight, natural, mined stuff. Moisten the two 'lites to cut down on dust, and mix them together in a big bucket or washtub or wheelbarrow or something *(do this outdoors and/or wear a dust mask 'cause it can still get dusty and you don't want to breathe a lot of any kind of dust)* with some nice finished compost. What with the moistening and the dust and the mixing and all, the dust mask's an even better idea now, as it will further that mad-scientist image you got going with the neighbors. If you don't have your own compost, you can buy it in a bag if you absolutely **have** to, but first try and bum some from a gardening friend: Homemade compost is the **best** compost!

> **That's: 1 part perlite**
> **1 part vermiculite**
> **1 part compost**

Or, if you're not opposed personally to using peat moss *(I'm not; some people think it's endangered, and I'm not going to judge what type you are— not about this anyway)*, you can make a very successful mix with equal parts of perlite, vermiculite, peat moss, and compost.

Be suspicious of all-in-one-bag mixes—even if they're labeled "seed-starting mix." If you don't make your own

If you must buy your "soil" all mixed up and ready in one bag, don't buy "potting soil." This term is often a synonym for lead and bricks mixed together in a bag.

FUTURE POTTING SOIL

mix, be sure to buy by weight, but in reverse: If the bag feels at all heavy for its size, pass! If the bag seems impossibly light for its size, you've got the right stuff. But be sure to check the label to see what's in that fluffy light bag. Some "mix makers" think they're doing you a favor by tossing in a little chemical fertilizer for your future seedlings. But "just say no." Your little 'maters don't need none of that extra "stuff" around their roots, no sir.

THE MAIN EVENT!

OK, now comes the fun part! Fill your containers with the seed-starting mix, leaving an inch or so of space at the top of the containers. But don't plant any seeds yet. First, put the containers into their dishes, pour water into the dishes, and go watch TV or something for an hour while the mix absorbs the water. If the dish is dry when you come back, add a little water and keep doing this until water just starts to pool up in the bottom of the dish. Then place **two seeds** in each 6-pack cell. If you're starting more than one variety, keep a chart of which variety is where *(don't use Popsicle sticks or other big plant markers yet)*. I put a different color twist-tie into the dirt of both center cells of each 6-pack and then draw a corresponding chart with the variety names and twist-tie color locations. That way you won't get confused when and if you move the 6-packs around.

Then cover the seeds with more of the mix; somewhere around a $1/2$ inch. You can mist the top of your freshly planted "seed bed" with a gentle *(and **clean**—nothing that had vinegar or anything other than water in it!)* sprayer, or just add a little more water to the bottom of the dish. Don't water from above with anything stronger than a mist—your seeds will wash away and you won't know what's where, and you'll be confused and discouraged, and you haven't even gotten anything really started yet.

Now cover the top of the whole shebang with a loose sheet of plastic wrap *(don't make it tight and clingy)* to help keep things moist. Then place this extremely professional setup some-place where it stays nice and warm—70° to 75°F is ideal. If you want guaranteed success, invest in one of those little seed-starting heating mats; it'll keep the temperature perfect for your tomatoes-to-be. Otherwise, the two generally best places in the average home are

> **1)** on top of the refrigerator, where the warm air from the compressor wafts up; or

> **2)** on top of the TV set, where,

once again, a gentle warm air rises out of. Or up from. Or something. *(Warning: Avoid this second option if you're in the habit of throwing things at your idiot box, or if yours isn't as flat-topped and stable as mine and your wet soil, seeds, and excess water might slide down the back of your TV right in the middle of your favorite "Hogan's Heroes" episode.)*

Examine your precious babies every day. Lift off the plastic to let them breathe a bit and check the moisture level of their "dirt."

If the top of the soil is obviously moist, don't do nothin'. Put the plastic back on top and put 'em back in their warm spot.

If it seems dry, give it a spritzin' or add a little water to the bottom of the holding tray. Don't go nuts; there shouldn't be water in the bottom of that dish all the time. That's **should NOT be,** OK?

In maybe 5 days, but certainly after a week or so, you should see the first sprouts push up out of the soil. Take the plastic off as soon as you see the first little green one pokin' up *(and DO savor the moment—isn't this great?! It's like a fabulous first date! Just don't think about the fights and credit card bills to come.)*, and get your lights ready.

After a week or so, you should see sprouts pushing up out of the soil. Yes, this will really happen. And yes, you will feel really good then. But don't get cocky.

27

THE LIGHTS

This is where most people fall down. Hard. Your young sprouts now need **LIGHT!** Good strong light to make them grow up thick and strong and stocky, and not like a 7-foot-5-inch basketball player who weighs 150 pounds. Provide too little light and that's what you will get—tall, spindly plants that are desperately trying to reach above the trees they feel they must be surrounded by.

And your so-called sunny windowsill hasn't gotten any less fatal in the past week or so.

Now, if you have the **perfect** windowsill—so heavily insulated that it **NEVER** gets too cold at night, **AND** you can gauge the exact perfect distance to place the plants away from the window so they don't get fried when the sun comes blasting in but still get enough light to grow up stocky, **AND** you keep that window clean on both sides, **AND** you turn the plants a quarter turn **AT LEAST** once every day . . .

C'mon—the shop light costs $10 when it's **NOT** on sale, and the 40-watt tubes'll cost ya a couple bucks more. And when your tamatas go out to the garden, you can put houseplants like African violets under it and make them happier than they've ever been. Or you could take it down to light your shop.

big seed-starting no-nos

Do **NOT** place your precious seedlings-to-be:

1. On top of a radiator or near any other source of extreme heat. Two words: Baked dirt.

2. On a "sunny windowsill." Put a thermometer there. I bet it cranks up to 90° something when the sun blazes in and drops to at least 50°F in the middle of the night. Not exactly the cozy-incubator effect we were looking for, eh?

Anyway, rig the light up with the chains that will doubtless accompany it so that you can raise it up as the plants grow, or start out with your setup resting on bricks or boards or something that you can remove as the plants grow. Because you want to keep the tops of your precious plants really close to those life-giving bulbs.

In the beginning, position your tender sprouts so that there's about an inch between them and the lights. That's a **REAL** inch, by the way, not a foot or 6 inches or even twoanahalf—you want these babies **CLOSE.** And as they grow taller and stronger, you want to maintain that 1-inch nearness to the lights. That's why we use fluorescents—the light they pro-duce is cool; the bulbs don't get hot and so don't harm the plants. Which is good 'cause the light intensity of the bulbs drops off sharply past an inch or so away, and you **HAVE** to keep plants and bulbs in each other's personal space to get fat *(OK—"stocky")*, happy, young tamatas.

Leave these lights on 24/7. If you can't do that, leave them on all the time. Really! Yes, I know most people would tell you to turn them off for 8 hours or so every night to simulate darkness, but, honey—darkness is the **LAST** thing those 'maters of yours need!

While these fluorescents do give off a nice shine o' light *(especially the lovely and talented four-tubers)*, they ain't no sun. That giant, constantly exploding, nuclear chain reaction in the sky that your plants will be *(eventually/hopefully/certainly)* enjoying all summer long is **HOT** and **BRIGHT,** and your plants will actually be very relieved when it goes down for a while after a cloudless day. Those fluorescent tubes hanging over your tomato babies are nowhere near as bright, and they ain't hot at all. Turn them off at night and you risk your plants getting "leggy" instead of "stocky"—desirable perhaps for people, but not for baby tomato plants. Bottom line: Make up for the fact that your lights ain't the sun by leaving them on alla time.

Those young starts will be grateful for the extra light—and don't worry, they'll do just fine when they finally experience night. Hey, up Alaska it don't get dark for months, and people up there don't develop early blight as a result. So there.

Oh, and you don't need to be keeping your plants especially warm anymo'. In the 60s is fine. Try not to let them get too hot or cold.

WE'RE ALMOST DONE!

The next month and a half will be your easiest in this adventure. The most important thing you have to do now is **NOT OVERWATER!**

NEWS FLASH:
OVERWATERING kills more plants than everything else combined!

Got that? Good. Now find a place where you can shimmy your little finger *(or a toothpick)* down an inch or so into your soil and check every other day or so. If it's dry a couple of inches down, then you can water— still from the bottom.

In fact, what I'd suggest here is that you do your watering by taking your dishes out to the sink, put water in them until it pools up, wait a half hour, pour out all the water still in bottom of the dish, and then return your well-soaked sprouts to their upright and under-the-light positions. Depending on your indoor humidity, you should only need to do this every 4 days to as long as a week.

'NOTHER NEWS FLASH:
DO NOT WATER EVERY DAY!
Your plants will rot and drown and die!
All plants like to dry out between waterings. **Be brave.**

SPEAKING OF BEING BRAVE . . .

We had you put two seeds into each cell because there's always the occasional bad seed that doesn't want to sprout. But you don't want to keep the two plants you'll now have in most of those little cells. Nope. Their widdle woots need woom to gwow. Only one plant in each pair is bound for your garden. Its slender cellmate must give its life for the greater good of the garden.

Get back here! Yes, you **have** to do this. And no, you can't just pull out the weaker one—you must **snip** it—their roots are already all wrapped up together, and you'll just pull the whole shebang out.

After you've gone and had a good cry, give the survivors their first feeding. Instead of just water, give them a nice drink of compost tea *(see "Compost Tea" on page 59)* or a very dilute *(half the strength it says on the label)* solution of a nice balanced organic fertilizer, like a seaweed concoction, a fish emulsion, or best of all, a mix of the two. This will now replace every other watering—that is, from here on in, when your babies need moisture, you should alternate between plain

Get a little pair of scissors and clip off the plant with the skinnier stalk to give the stockier seedling more room.

ol' water and dilute liquid fertilizer *(like compost tea)*. Pour off any extra fertilizing liquid into your houseplants or on your roses outside or something.

COUNTDOWN TO GREATNESS!

If you've gotten this far and have a nice-looking crop of young plants, you're over the hump, baby! Keep them under those lights, water sparingly, and start planning your outdoor placement—'cause as soon as they're old enough *(6 to 8 weeks)* and it stays warm enough *(nighttime temps that are mostly in the 50s; some high 40s are okay, but nothing colder—you'll just be rushing the poor babies)*, we're going outside!

Whoo! Oh, I'm just SO excited!!!!

the Art of Tomato Planting

(You want me to BURY them? You MONSTER!!)

By now you should have either nice, stocky 6- to 8-week-old tomato plants you started yourself from seed or some plants of unknown origin you bought at a garden center 'cause you were too chicken to try what I told you last chapter. *(If that is the case, don't worry—it's all right; we don't judge.)*

"HEY EVERYBODY!!! *(Your Name Here)* **BOUGHT HER TOMATOES ALREADY STARTED!!!!"**

Well, OK—maybe we **DO** judge just a little. But you'll start with seed **NEXT** year, right? Don't make me have to write a Second Edition to yell at you again.

Now, as I said, you **should** have tomato plants at the ready right now. If you **DON'T,** you must stop reading **RIGHT NOW** and purchase some nice "stocky" *(which sounds so much nicer than "short and fat," but that's what it means and that is indeed what you want—at least in tomato plants)* plants before proceeding, or I'll send the people who make sure you don't skip ahead on the SATs and other college entrance exams after you. And those big rulers of theirs **HURT.**

We will now do a number of things simultaneously. Or if you can't manage simultaneously, we'll do them all at the same time.

HARDENING OFF (your plants, that is!)

This is actually very important—*especially* if you started your own plants from seed. What we want to do here is get those puppies gradually acclimated to the conditions outdoors *(which are colder, damper, and basically more treacherous in every way possible than the wonderfully controlled indoor weather you've been providing. And no—you CAN'T just keep them indoors with you. They're tomatoes, not cats.).*

Keep an eye on the weather and look for a stretch where mild temperatures are expected to prevail for several days in a row and not be immediately followed by a raging blizzard. If it's going to stay really nasty out for a while, don't worry about what the calendar says or how many weeks old your plants are—put this part off. Better to let them get a little overgrown than freeze to death, drown, or otherwise join The Choir Invisible. Putting them out into nasty cold weather because you're afraid it's getting too late in the season has **nothing** going for it. Unprotected tomatoes will just sit there *(if you're lucky and they don't kick the bucket outright)* and refuse to grow until temps warm up.

OK—let's say we got a nice day coming up with a prediction of decent weather the week after. Put your tomato plants outside for an hour or two. Then bring them back in. The next day, leave them out a little longer. Same for the next day. Depending on the weather and your tolerance for this kind of thing, you will soon leave them out overnight. This should **not** be a night where it is expected to be really chilly, rainy, or the like. And **snow** is totally out!

Yes, this seems tedious, but this specific act of tediousness provides bigger rewards than most of the other tedious stuff you gotta do in life. In fact, if you ignore my advice and just plant the suckers right there in the ground straight from the house, all your pretty little tomato plants will lie down and take long nappies. Perhaps forever, depending on just how poor your judgment and the weather are.

Take your tomato plants outside and let them enjoy the outdoors for an hour or two. Then bring them back in, and say "Nice tomato plants! Good tomato plants!"

Tamatas that are not hardened-off go into shock. It's kind of like when you were born—you left that warm little liquid bubble where you just floated blissfully and nothing bothered you for so long and then—**BOOM!** You're surrounded by bright lights, loud noises, and a guy in a mask slapping your keister. No wonder you cried. And you've never quite gotten over it, have you?

Don't do this to your tomatoes.

Wouldn't it have been nice if your mom had given you a little peek at the outside world, at your older brothers and sisters who were gearing up to spend the rest of their lives tormenting you, and at all the other nice things that awaited your entrance, and then popped you back in for awhile and eased you out gradually over the course of

34

a week or so? Well, you can do for your tomatoes what your mom was too selfish to do for you!

By letting your plants get used to the outdoors gradually, you'll prevent them from experiencing transplant shock. And your reward will be bigger, happier, healthier plants that will grow faster, produce more tasty tomatoes, and be better able to naturally resist disease and pest attacks all summer long.

They won't die right away, either. That's always a plus.

LOCATION, LOCATION, LOCATION

Tomatoes really are among the easiest plants you can grow—that's one reason why so many folks grow 'em *(all the other reasons are related to the grower's ethnic background and/or the nonflavor of supermarket tomatoes)*. But they are also plants that are native to a region where their leaves almost never get wet. When we grow 'em here, our rain and general dampness makes them prone to certain diseases. You can **greatly limit**—perhaps even prevent—such problems by choosing a spot to grow your love apples that is not conducive to disease.

Actually make that **spotS.** If you have—or are planning—a nice big garden with lots of different foods and flowers, don't group all your similar plants of any one kind in one spot. If, for instance, you have eight tomato plants and eight raised beds, I suggest you place one plant in each bed instead of filling up, say, two of the beds with all your tomato plants **because:**

Many of your finer tomatoes—including all of your heirlooms and big beefsteak, sandwich types—grow on big **honking** plants that no one ever gives enough room to. Many is the time that I've pulled up a depleted

10-foot-or-more *Brandywine* or *Mortgage Lifter* vine at the end of the season only to discover that *that's* where that missing hot pepper, cucumber, or eggplant was! Plant a whole bunch of tomatoes in one bed and you risk crowding your plants together so much that they will soon become one giant tangled heap of vines that can't dry out and are just begging for disease to come calling. So plant them apart *and* plant them apart: Don't group them all together, **AND** plan to leave plenty of room between your tomatoes and other large plants *(put lettuce and spinach and little flowers around them; it won't hurt, and it'll look pretty)*.

Grouping all of your plants of the same type together lends a helping hand to pests and diseases. Once a bad bug or plant sickness finds one of your tomatoes, it will have found them all, and it will then spread its negative effects faster than a bad winter cold in a day-care center where nobody washes their hands. And believe it or not, research studies have found that simply mixing up your plantings confuses and discourages garden pests.

WE'RE ALMOST THERE

If you plan your garden this way, take notes when you plant so you can remember **where** in each bed you planted your tomatoes. Maybe make it easy and plant your tomatoes on the left-hand side of each bed, for instance, or mark the spot with a circle of Popsicle sticks or the cutworm collar can I'll soon describe. Then, next year, plant your tomatoes at the opposite end of each bed, and the following year in the middle. You want to avoid planting tomatoes *(and many other crops, but especially tomatoes)* in the same spot each season; otherwise, soilborne diseases like verticillium and fusarium wilt will take hold and attack your plants.

And if you're a lucky person who has lots of gardening room *(I'll try not to dislike you for this, since I got a postage stamp surrounded by woods)*, you can **position** your plants perfectly as well. "Perfect" is where they will get the first possible rays of the morning sun. Morning sun burns off nighttime dampness quickly, and a dry tomato plant is a happy tomato plant. Conversely *(like the Chuck Taylor sneakers I used to wear back in high school)*, if your plants have to wait until the afternoon to dry off, they'll be miserable, prone to disease, and may report you to the police. Corn and cabbages couldn't care less about morning sun. Hostas don't need **ANY** sun. But tomato plants *(and roses)* love and need morning rays.

So—once again, before we digs a hole, we wants to makes sure:

Think of afternoon sun this way: You get out of a nice heated swimming pool into the cool air of the morning and someone brings you a nice dry towel 4 hours later. Was that good for you?

■ the plants won't be crowded when they reach full size *(which is roughly 6,000 times bigger than they are now, give or take a hundredfold or so)*;

■ they aren't all grouped together *(unless you deliberately want to plant them all in one or two **BIG HUMONGOUSLY LARGE** beds so you can rotate them to different beds next year, ensuring that you won't follow tomatoes with tomatoes. I'll let you go on this—in fact, it can be a good strategy—but only if you give each plant lots of room!)*; and

■ they're in the spot in the garden that gets the most and earliest morning sun and are out in the open with good air circulation all around *(don't plant them up against a wall or where they'll be surrounded by other tall plants)*.

Yes, I do realize that in the real world, few people can achieve **all** of these things. But what I have described *is* the ideal situation, and the closer you get to it, the happier we'll all be. For instance: Can't manage morning sun? Then make **sure** that the plants are out in the open, with good air circulation all around. And don't worry—you're going to do just fine and have fun doing it. This is not a test. It is an artistic experience, and you **will** enjoy what you get out of it.

Unless all your plants die, of course. *(Did I mention that yet?)*

Anyway, now that we've got the site picked out, we're **finally** ready to plant. OK—**almost** ready. Hey, don't worry—things get moving pretty quickly after this. It's like house painting, where it takes you 2 weeks to scrape, peel, clean, spackle, sand, apply masking tape, and otherwise prepare the surface, and about 20 minutes to actually fling the paint on. Preparation is everything. And remember what the wall looked like when you **didn't** scrape, spackle, peel, and clean, and you ran out of masking tape and used Scotch tape instead? You don't ever want to see that again, do you?

MAKING YOUR SOIL SLIGHTLY LESS LOUSY

If your soil is already compost-enriched and nice and loose and all, you may skip down to "Burying Your Plants with Gabige" on page 41. If, however, you are among the other 96 percent of the population and have really lousy soil, you should improve it first. Whether lousy through clay, lousy through sand, or just plain lousy, a little bit of "double-digging" can do wonders for poor soil. Strenuous but not complicated, double-digging is little more than taking a lot of dirt out of the ground and then putting it back in again. Yes, it does sound remarkably like Army work, but the process really loosens up the soil and allows your tomato plants' roots to breathe and reach down deep for moisture and nutrients. This is especially important if, like I here in Pennsylvania *(an old Native American word that means "so much clay in the soil you can make terra-cotta pots just by spinning your hand in the ground")*, you have a lot of heavy clay.

DOUBLE-DIGGING 101

First, dig a trench across the area you want to plant in, about a foot or so wide and just as deep. If you're growing in raised beds *(which I would explain in depth, but if I do that, we'll* **NEVER** *gets these puppies in the ground; besides, I need stuff to write future books about. I hope.)*, you'll want to double-dig the whole bed, of course. Toss the removed soil into a wheelbarrow or onto a tarp, removing rocks and any large, obvious hunks of pure clay as you go. Then get a digging fork *(a garden, not a kitchen, tool)* or other long, strong spikey thing and jab it into the ground at the bottom of the hole repeatedly. Feel free to think of someone "special" if this will increase your jabbing time and/or intensity. Now repeat this the length of the bed or row, filling in each prepared trench with the newly removed soil from the next one.

When you're done moving and spiking it all, bust up the soil in the wheelbarrow or tarp with the side of a shovel or a hoe and use that to fill in the last trench. Toss all of the rocks and big chunks of clay away. They will not make your tomatoes happy. And don't feel bad—after 15 years of double-digging and literally **tons** of added compost, I still find enough clods of clay in my garden beds every season to supply a college pottery class for several semesters. If you wind up with not a lot of soil left, that's great—now you got room to put some *good* stuff into that trench.

(If, for some strange reason, double-digging lacks appeal for you, use a rotary tiller. A power tiller is especially useful if you have a big garden,

39

you can't double-dig personally, and/or you leap at every excuse to operate power equipment. Make sure the soil is nice and dry—otherwise it'll clump up in unpleasantly irreversible ways, and you'll kill lots of earthworms. Contrary to popular opinion, an earthworm sliced in half does **not** *yield two happy littler worms. In fact, it rarely yields one live worm— and he's never happy about it. When the soil is nice and dry, the worms won't be there.)*

Now, back to putting in the good stuff. Like compost. The compost you make yourself from shredded leaves, dried grass clippings, and nonmeat kitchen gabige is the best possible amendment you can add to your soil.

get **smart** about compost

Don't use compost made with treated sewage sludge (a.k.a. "biosolids")—too many morons and criminals still pour industrial chemicals, motor oil, and the like down their terlets and into the sewers, ruining what otherwise would be nice stuff to grow in. Compost in a bag is acceptable but not nearly as good as homemade, municipal, or mushroom soil. Bulk compost from places with big piles of nice-looking stuff sitting outside is probably OK. Here's how to tell for sure:

- It should look like rich, black "super-soil."

- It should have no "off" or foul odors; it can smell a little sweet or earthy, but nothing that makes your nose turn up.

- It should not contain any recognizable wood chips or other "original ingredients."

- When you pick some up in your hand and squeeze it, it should have the consistency of a damp, wrung-out sponge.

- Lots of worms living in it are a very good sign.

The only thing better is homemade compost bummed from a fellow gardener *(because you didn't have to make it).*

Next best is aged mushroom soil *(a.k.a. mushroom compost, spent mushroom soil, etc.)* purchased in bulk. Or look for municipal compost made from fall leaves and horse manure from stables, like the city of Philadelphia and many other municipalities provide free to their residents. If your city or township has a place to take yard wastes for recycling, you can probably get free compost there because that's what they recycle the stuff into. Take home **lots** of this "black gold" for your garden. Get some for me while you're there.

Alright—mix lots of that fine compost into your loosened-up soil. Now look up to the sky like a farmer in a big-screen movie. The music swells. The clouds part. A ray of sunshine strikes the very spot you've improved so well. You're ready to plant. Life is good.

BURYING YOUR PLANTS WITH GABIGE

OK—we be planting! First, suck in your gut, breathe from your toes, and summon all the courage you can because you are about to come very close to burying your poor charges alive. Really. Tomatoes will develop auxiliary roots along any part of their stem that is buried. This is good. Those extra roots can reach **lots** more water and nutrients than the roots of an unburied plant, and they also help anchor the plant in the ground. When I plant, I bury the bottom three-quarters of my tomato starts under ground. Just the top 4 inches or so left up top. **Trust me.**

There are two different ways to do this:

1. In really cold climates: You will bury your stems "trench-style" *(Italian gardeners will do this as well, even if they live in Texas; they can't* *help themselves—and besides, they're Italian and so their tomatoes will grow beautifully no matter what they do).* Dig your hole, then fill it almost to the top with your loosened-up soil mixed with compost, add your crushed-up eggshells *(see "The Eggshell Thing" on the opposite page),* and then lay the plant stem down horizontally on top of the soil and **gently** bend the last 4 inches or so straight up. Cover the to-be-buried section with at least 2 inches *(4 would be ideal)* of your soil mix. You are following this procedure because your cold soil takes forever to warm up in the spring, especially down deep. By placing the rooted section close to the surface, you keep it in the warmest possible soil while still getting the benefits of the buried stem.

2. In warmer climates: You don't have to trench. In fact, the warmer the region you are gardening in, the less you should trench because **YOUR** tomatoes' roots will **ENJOY** wiggling around in as **cool** a soil as possible. So fill in your hole with loosened soil and compost until you can place the rootball of the plant against the bottom of the hole and have just a few inches of plant out in the world. Put the plant in the hole and fill it in with more soil and compost and some eggshells *(see "The Eggshell Thing"; hey—didn't you read the previous "cold clime" paragraph? Not even out of curiosity? You* **paid** *for it all!* **Read** *it all!),* tamping it down **lightly.** Don't go nuts with the tamping! **NO** plant likes compacted soil!

Note: To get your plants safely out of their containers *(like plastic nursery 6-packs),* squeeze the outside of each container gently all around until the plant and its soil will slide or pop out easily. Don't disturb that big clump of soil around the roots! Place it gently against the bottom of your hole *(or sideways if you're cold and/or Italian)* and fill in around it.

THE EGGSHELL THING:
McG'S SUPER TOMATO-GROWING SECRET #1!

Tomatoes need calcium. I firmly believe that adequate soil calcium produces the best-tasting fruits and helps avoid one of the biggest bummers of tomato growers everywhere—blossom-end rot. Long wet spells, long dry spells, and/or alternating drought and flood can cause the fruits to go bad on the bottom.

Somebody told me a long time ago to save up all my eggshells *(or make friends with somebody who works in a restaurant that serves breakfast)*. Let them air-dry *(just 24 hours or so and they're nice and crumbly)*, and then add the crushed-up shells of a dozen or so eggs to each planting hole wherein you hope to achieve tomato happiness.

I can *assure* you that this works **great!** In fact, its greatness has just been personally reaffirmed this past season in my very own garden! I'm a born-again eggshell proselytizer!

Before this season *(the most recent one my garden endured before I wrote this)*, I had started to wonder if I had perhaps been fooling myself all these years, and if the Eggshell Thing **really** mattered. But I had saved **tons** of eggshells already, **and** it had been raining all spring, so I added a buncha crushed shells to each hole, and then it *really* started raining and never stopped. By August, everybody else's tomatoes looked **awful**—lots of blossom-end rot especially—while mine were the hands-down prettiest I've ever grown. *(I also spaced them farther away from other plants than usual—the Magic Eight Ball told me to, and it was right.)*

So air-dry the shells of a dozen eggs *(they really do turn bone-dry in just a day or so)*, crush 'em up real fine, and mix 'em into the soil right around the roots. Don't believe me? Try it with a few plants and leave the others shell-free. I guarantee you'll eat lots of eggs the winter after the results are in.

CHAPTER 4

Staking and Caging

(No, *not* "or," "AND"! Got it?! "Staking AND Caging"!!!)

OK—you got your babies in the ground. Now you have to build them a house they can grow up in. And grow they will—like teenage boys on a diet of cheeseburgers and single-serving half-gallon ice cream cartons! We're talking size 18 shoes by the middle of July, ladies and gentlemen. If you don't prepare for that growth now, woe will be yours!

And wouldn't you really rather have tomatoes than woe? I know I would.

Yes, it's time to stake **and** cage those teeny-tiny plants, despite their current teeny-tinyness because they ain't gonna be teeny-tiny for long *(hopefully, anyway, and don't ask for your money back if they are. It wasn't* **my** *fault! It was* **your** *fault!* **You** *did it!)*. Sorry.

Anyway, yes—you **have** to do this. **Two reasons:**

1. Tomatoes are vines. Or rather, tomatoes grow **on** vines. Either way, they ain't trees, honey. Left to their own devices, your tomato plants will just flop right down onto the soil. Laying *(lying? prone?)* on the ground like that makes it virtually impossible for the plants to get good air circulation, thus making them very susceptible to diseases and just plain rotting from being on the wet ground. They'll get all dirty, too.

That's why most people **at least** "stake" their tomatoes. No, **not** like the fruits are little green vampires! Put down that sharp stick! I mean driving an 8-foot stake **deep** into the ground *(leaving at least 5 or 6 feet above-ground)* and then **gently** *(and continually, as the plant grows)* securing the main tomato vine to that stake with something that won't cut into the vine and sever it under pressure *(for example,* **NOT** *fishing line or piano wire).*

Unsupported tomato vines will crawl along the ground, where slugs and other dastardly creatures will take one big bite (and only one) out of each of your love apples, ruining the harvest and your chance for a happy life, slim as that was to begin with.

Fishing line and piano wire are exceptionally poor choices for tying up tomatoes. Twist-ties can be risky as well because they have wire inside. Strips of soft cloth or foam or a commercial "tie-your-tomatoes-up" bondage product would be best.

But I'm not recommending that you live by stake alone. Nope—those stakes can give way to harsh weather/really heavy plants, and I always worry about too much pressure on the vine at the tie points no matter how silken the bonds. On top of that, you have to remember to constantly keep up with the new growth during the season *(and anything involving memory is a big "no" at our house. What was I saying?)*. No—we're going to use **our** stakes to hold our **cages** in place. Because we're special. Yes, we are.

2. As mentioned previously, your little plants that are now just inches tall will grow like the dickens and become very tall. And gangly. Just like those aforementioned teenage boys. The vines of a big heirloom tomato plant *(like* Brandywine, Jefferson Giant, Georgia Streak, Mortgage Lifter . . . *)* can reach 10 feet in length. And while we **do** want lots of air-flow around the leaves, we probably also want to grow a few other plants in this garden, so these giants need to be contained. And, as Carl Denham* proved so well in that Broadway show he did with the big gorilla from Skull Island back in the '30s, chains are simply not enough. You need a cage.

So what we're gonna do is surround these teeny-tiny, barely visible little plants with a **big honkin' cage.** And we're gonna support that cage

*Remember his immortal line from *King Kong* (1933): "There's no reason to worry! Those chains are made of chrome steel!"

with a nice sturdy 6-foot-high *(or more)* stake, driven a couple of feet into the ground. The stake will prevent the cage from falling over in high winds and heavy rains and also from being dragged down by the overwhelming weight and size of the fully grown plant that will soon be drooping and pulling all over it. Tomatoes are not pumpkins *(the true 300-pound gorillas of the garden)*, but some of those big heirlooms come darn close.

The plant will somewhat climb up the inside of the cage as it grows, and then stop close to or at the top *(determinate varieties)* or continue growing *(indeterminate varieties)*, spill over the top of the cage, and grow back down again. If it reaches the ground, you can start: **a)** trimming it by cutting the new growth off; **b)** training the vines over to the next cage; **c)** tying the vines sideways to relatively open *(ha!)* sections of the cage; or **d)** running screaming for the hills in fear.

Let us now pause for a word about those pre-made conical 2-foot-high "tomato cages" sold in hardware stores and garden centers in the spring:

HA!

Those are not cages, my friend. If we define a cage as being something like the structures that prevent leopards at the zoo from having the visitors for breakfast, then those little "tomato cage" cones are jars with holes in the lids for catching lightning bugs on a hot summer night.

Now, I **do** actually own some of those tomato cages myself. I use them to support big-fruited bell pepper plants like *California Wonder* and *Fat & Sassy (yes, I realize what a straight line that last variety name is, but this is a* **tomato** *book).* To use one of them little thangs to support a tomato plant would be like trying to tow a truck with kite string. A **big** truck. And the string came from the Dollar Store.

MAKING CAGES

You want to buy a roll of STURDY 4- or 5-foot-high, welded-wire **fencing.** *Not* chicken wire. You can make a darn good compost bin out of chicken wire. **DARN** good. You can also roll chicken wire out flat on the fluffy, loose soil of your raised beds to deter kitty cats who are mistaking those beds for litter boxes. *(You can seed crops like lettuce and spinach and such right through the flattened fencing; use tin snips to cut holes in it for tomato and pepper transplants and the like—works great!)* But you can't use it to cage tomatoes. It's not rigid enough, and you can't reach through them tiny little openings to pick *(ripe tomatoes and/or slugs and/or hornworms off your tomatoes).*

So your fencing needs to be sturdy **AND** have big enough openings that you can squeeze a hand through when necessary. *(Those openings don't have to be large enough to pass all your future tomatoes thru, however—you probably will be able to do that with your paste and cherry tomatoes, but most of the big boys will have to be reached down for or if they're really low, be handed up the inside of the fencing like at the ballpark when all those people closer to the aisle get to handle your hot dog before it gets to you in the middle of the row.)*

Any large hardware store or garden center will have a good variety of choices *(often labeled "animal fencing" or "rabbit fencing" or the like)* in 50-foot-long rolls, from which you can make 8 to 10 cages. I bought a couple of rolls of fairly generic fencing for about 20 bucks a roll over a decade ago, and the cages are still in great shape *(OK—they're really rusty but still structurally sound).* However, I retired them recently because I found something really spiffy to use instead. *(OK—and because they really got rusty over the years. What are you—a cop??)*

It's called "Gard'n Fence" *(yes! I saved the wrapper!)*. It's made in Italy, is 4 feet high, comes in a 50-foot roll, and has 2 × 3-inch openings in the mesh, which are a **little** small for my hands, but the fencing is nicely flexible, so I can easily bend a little extra into the top and bottom of a section *(making it closer to 4 × 3)* and then squeeze my hand through to pick and/or pass the ripe ones out. I was first attracted to this roll of fencing by the color—a beautiful dark green. The actual metal of the fencing is entirely coated with a layer of green vinyl, which means that it won't rust like my old cages *(or maybe it will, but we won't see it because the rust would be under that coating)*. It looked like it would make really nice tomato cages in the store, and it certainly has.

Nine of 'em, in fact. All somewhat different in size, which I strongly urge you to do as well. *(Note big space-saving tip on this page.)*

I start out by making a couple cages out of 6-foot-long sections, then some out of 5½-foot-long sections, then 5 feet, etc. *(Start to keep track of what's left when you've got say, six cages done, so you don't end up with a 3-foot-long section from which you could only make a giant spitball tube.)* My biggest honkin' heirloom plants go into the 6-footers *(which have a finished diameter of around 22 or 23 inches)*, my compact paste tomato varieties go into the smallest cages *(5-foot lengths; a diameter of 17 to 18 inches)*, and then I attempt to predict final sizes to fit what's left. That's one of the things I really love about gardening: Most of the questions are multiple choice **and** essay, all at the same time.

big space-saving **tip:**

When I make my tomato cages, I try and vary them enough in size so that, when the season is over, I can stack two or three smaller ones inside each really big one, so that there's a prayer they won't eat up all our *(meager, like yours)* storage room.

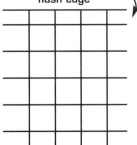

cut for attaching to flush edge

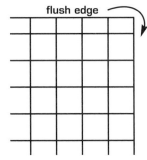

flush edge

HOW TO MAKE TOMATO CAGES

Get a helper, a good pair of leather gloves for both *(each?)* of youse *(make sure everybody's got gloves, OK?)*, and a pair of tin snips. Assemble on a nice flat surface, like a driveway.

Measure out 6 feet *(or other length of your choice)* of fencing, have your helper hold it down/out, and cut it off the roll with your tin snips so that one end of this cut section will have "loose" pieces of fencing sticking out all along the cut edge. The edge of what's left on the roll should be "flush," like the end of the roll itself before you started. This part is important; look at the picture over there! You want to be sure and cut it this way because those "stick-out" spokes are going to hold your cage together.

Now shape the fencing into a circle and use those natural, twist-tie–like spokes to attach one side to the other—just wrap them around the edges of the little openings on the flush side until they're secure and no sharp edges are protruding. This will give you a much more secure structure than if you tried to use string, wire, twist-ties, or whatever to hold the edges together. *Your* connectors are part of the actual fencing, and there's nothing stronger.

Now look at the bottom of the fencing *(Which end is the bottom? Your choice!* **You** *decide which end will rest in the doit and which shall strain toward the sky! Don't abuse this awesome power!)*; it is likely one nice continuous piece of wire fencing stuff. Not for long. Take your tin snips and cut one side of the very bottom of every third or fourth little rectangular opening (**NOT** *all of them—just a few of them, evenly spaced)* so that you can straighten out each of those little still-attached pieces of wire and point them downward, making little positioning stakes.

Now position your assembled cage so that the ridiculously small tomato you expect to be the biggest honking one in your garden *(assuming you made* a big 6-foot cage like I told ya to) come July is in the center *(if you want to use a cutworm collar, put it on there now; see "Block That Pest!" on page 53).* Shove the cage into the ground so those little stakes you made in the bottom go allaway into the soil. Now remove the cage for a second and cover the area between the plant and those little holes well with your mulch. *(See "Your Mulch Choices" on page 54.)* Then put the cage into place for real.

Take your big long stake and position it in the back of the cage, where it will be behind the tomato plant when the plant is full-grown and thus hidden from view. Make sure it's nice and flush up against the fencing. Pound it down a good 2 feet into the ground. Then, when it will be pounded no more, secure it to the cage. You can do this with wire or heavy-duty twist-ties, but I like to just slip the top of the stake through one of the openings in the cage and then bend that fencing material back and down around the stake. Holds well that way.

You've done it! Caged a tomato! It won't get far now!

Now continue making cages out of the rest of the roll. The exact sizes are up to you—and depend, of course, on what kind of plants you'll be growing. If they're all going to be **BIG HONKIN'** heirlooms *(and cage storage isn't an issue)*, just make eight big ones, each using a smidge more than 6 feet of fencing. All compact paste tomatoes? Make ten 5-footers out of that 50-foot roll.

If you're compulsive and need a finite plan, here's a good one for a 50-foot roll:

4 cages made using 6-foot lengths = 24 feet of fencing
2 cages made using 5½-foot lengths = 11 feet of fencing
3 cages made using 5-foot lengths = 15 feet of fencing
Total: 9 cages made using 50 feet of fencing

AMAZING! *(I think this is pretty much what I did this year, actually.)*

Don't worry—
growing tomatoes is like
raising children: Perfection
on your part is simply not
possible. You're GOING to
screw up, but they'll
probably be just fine
anyway as long
as you tried to do
your best and
didn't call
them "stupid."
Too often.

A final word on parenting/tomatoing: Caging and staking your young, tiny tomatoes is like reading to your children before they're old enough to possibly understand anything you're saying. It may look foolish to others, but it gets your loved ones off to a great start. *(Just don't confuse which to read to and which to cage.)*

A FEW WORDS ABOUT CUTWORMS

It has never happened to me personally, but I've heard from many gardeners who **have** suffered the heartbreak of *Cutwormariasus.* You come out to the garden one bright and hopeful morning early in the season and your young tomato transplants *(and other garden crops as well)* are lying on their sides, separated cleanly from their life-sustaining roots, which are still stuck tight in the soil.

The nasty larval form of a useless but otherwise harmless moth, cutworms are the worst kind of garden pests. My insect specialist buddy Dr. Linda Gilkeson describes it as "a fat, greasy caterpillar" in the excellent *Rodale's Pest & Disease Problem Solver (a book that allows you to look up in wretched living color all the creatures and diseases that have eaten and/or infected your garden).* Cutworms kill only young plants—i.e., your beautiful, wonderful, hope-for-the-future transplants of spring. Perhaps even more insulting, they don't even eat them! At least not right away. Apparently, cutworms sever transplants at the soil line so that the young plants will topple over and the vile, greasy little creature can later consume them without much effort. This slacker tactic of plant predation may work well in the wild, but in the home garden setting, all it does is destroy the faith in human nature of hundreds of novice gardeners each year, as they discover their young charges leveled one morning and then find themselves thinking back to the strange remark their next-door neighbor made the day before . . . .

SO I'M A CUTWORM. YOU GOT A PROBLEM WITH THAT?

If this happens to you, snoop around the scene of the crime a bit. You will probably find a cutworm or two *(or 20)* curled up next to a severed plant

block that **pest!**

It's really easy to thwart cutworms. Just make a circle of relatively hard material and shove it into the dirt around the young transplant. Your established options include:

■ Tin cans without either lid. Remove both ends of a soup-can–size can and insert the steel *(yes, I knew that they haven't been made of tin for some time now, thank you)* cylinder over the transplant, sinking it 1 or 2 inches into the soil.

■ A plastic soda bottle. Cut the top and bottom off of a 1- or 2-liter bottle and use as above.

■ Magazine response cards. Open up any magazine and then pick up the 600 or so little cards that drop out into your lap, take the biggest ones, fold them over into circles, and use as above. If, however, you catch the cutworms filling in the cards and trying to subscribe to, say, *Prevention* or *Bug's Health*, quickly move your family to another state.

or just under the surface of the soil. Feel free to exact revenge if you do *(in fact, we insist)*. But 'tis better to avoid the problem completely by using cut-worm collars when you plant. You should especially consider doing so if:

■ your young transplants have suffered such damage in the past *(Now aren't you sorry you put that burning bag of dog doo on your neighbor's porch to get even last year?)*;

■ you're planting a garden for the first time, don't know what to expect, and want to be careful *(insurance is always worth it, sez me)*;

■ you didn't cultivate the soil a lot at the end of last season and/or within the last month before planting *(doing so exposes the young destructoids to wonderful uncaring hungry birds)*; or

■ I've made you so paranoid that you won't be able to sleep otherwise.

YOUR MULCH CHOICES

You may want to surround your young transplants with something that will prevent weed growth before you cage them, although I don't do this *(for a reason I will soon reveal)* and still find it fairly easy to weed throughout the season.

Reason for not mulching: Slugs! In a wet and shady area *(or season)*, slugs can become an intolerable garden pest. There are many ways to fight them: beer, sharp sticks, diatomaceous earth, salt, copper, vinegar, small-caliber handguns, and the laying down of boards as traps. But cutting back on mulch can also be a **huge** help. Now don't get me wrong—a thick layer of weed-suppressing, moisture-conserving, soil-cooling mulch is one of the basic tenets of organic gardening. Unfortunately, it also gives slugs a place to hide during the day. So, if like **moi,**

you must garden in a sun-challenged site and/or a region where perpetual moistness be the norm, forgo the mulch and simply pull weeds as they appear.

However, the rest of youse—especially those who garden in full sun and/or in a really hot locale, and **especially** where it generally don't rain none *(like Arizona)*—**must** mulch. You need to keep your soil moisture as even as possible, and you probably don't have to worry about slugs *(it's OK: I'll send you some of mine. Autographed.)*.

Use shredded leaves *(**Not** WHOLE ones! Really—it's worth the effort!)*, dried grass clippings, straw, or the like. Don't mulch directly against the stem of the plant; pile it on from, say, 3 inches out all the way to the edge of the cage, a couple of inches deep.

If disease has been a problem in your patch, you can't rotate your tomatoes to different locations any more, and you want to stave off the symptoms until as late in the season as possible, use pure, fresh, finished compost alone as a mulch. It won't really hold down weeds, but it **will** feed your plants brilliantly *(you like that? "Brilliantly?" I like that. I oughta do this for a living . . .)*, **and** an inch layer of compost on top of the soil around your plants is the best hedge against disease. Apply a fresh $1/2$ inch or so of compost every 2 months afterward during the growing season *(and promptly remove and destroy any discolored leaves on your plants and off the ground as well—that's how disease* **really** *spreads)*.

Oh, and don't let all this "disease talk" scare you. Tomatoes **are** tropical **but** native to a **very** dry region *(Peru)*, where there's plenty of water **underground** but very little to wet their leaves aboveground. So they are more prone to plant diseases here where their leaves get wet a lot. But you're going to do just fine. **Really.** You can stop gripping the book so hard now.

CHAPTER 5

Food, Water, and Basic Keeping-Alive Skills

(Oops—you mean I *shouldn't* have watered them each and every day?)

If you've come even remotely close to doing what we've suggested thus far, the next couple of months should be a breeze. This really **IS** like house painting, where the actual time spent slapping the paint on seems infinitesimal compared to the hours and hours of laborious cleaning and prep work that you did beforehand. And if you've done **everything** we've suggested, the only purpose of this chapter will be to warn you not to overwater. Really.

I firmly believe that it is people trying to do too much for their tomatoes that kills the largest number of developing love apple starts in America today. **THEY'RE PLANTS, PEOPLE! NOT PREMATURE BABIES!** *(Unless, of course, you **really** screwed up on the germination chapter, and your little green charges are still in incubators being attended to by ICU nurses . . .)*

Seriously, if you got your plants off to a good start, buried 'em deep, fed 'em eggshells, mixed some compost into their loosened-up soil, gave 'em plenty of space, mulched 'em well, and all that other stuff you didn't do, you can just kick back for the next couple of months. Unless drought strikes. Then you have to wake up and water some. Got it?

OK? Great! Then let's move on to our next chapter—potential pest and disease problems!

I **said,** "Let's move on . . . " OK? C'mon—what are you hanging back here for? . . . What? You don't believe me? Alright, alright:

"FEEDING" YOUR TAMATAS

Like that guy in *The Graduate*, I got one word for you *(and it ain't "plastic")*. It's **compost.**

Back in Chapter 3, I urged you to mix some compost in with your soil when you loosened it up. If you did indeed mix in some of this priceless *(actually you can buy it pretty cheap)* soil amendment, you really shouldn't feed your plants anything else for a while. *(Then, about halfway through the season, you*

We're talking the King and Queen of Garden Nutrients! (I'm either the Jack or the Joker—hard to tell; they dress so much alike.)

can feed 'em more compost.) If, however, you *only* loosened up your soil *(or even worse, just plunged your poor plants into pretty much unamended rock-hard or cruddy, sandy soil)*, then yes, you **do** need to add some compost right now. No! Not later! Now! No—I **don't** care what time it is!

If you're reading this before the actual planting process *(and who **said** you could skip ahead? Did you bring a note?!)* and don't expect disease to be a significant problem *(because you haven't grown tomatoes in this spot before, and you have enough garden space to ensure good airflow between the full-grown plants, and they'll get good amounts of morning sun)*, go ahead and mix the compost into the soil before you start planting.

How much? Ideally, an amount that would equal a $1/2$- to 1-inch layer on top of about a 2 × 2-foot *(4 square feet)* plot of soil *(my approximation of the "footprint" of the average full-grown tomato plant)*. If you feel the need to measure **something** *(and Lord knows, you'll have precious few chances to do so in **this** book)*, go ahead and spread out $1/2$ to 1 inch of compost on top of a 2 × 2 area in the center of which you shall soon plant. Then mix it up with the soil that's already there *(minus rocks and clay clods, of course)*.

If the plant is already in the ground, simply spread $1/2$ to 1 inch of compost all around it, covering that 2 × 2 area *(feel free to extend it out even further for really big plants)*, and then place mulch *(like shredded leaves or straw)* over the compost to keep weeds down. Again, unless you expect disease to be a problem—then put the compost down **on top of** the mulch even if you already mixed the compost into the soil itself. That layer of compost is like a force field against disease.

58

COMPOST TEA

Now, I'm a realist. I **know** you have a burning desire to **feed** and *(you believe)* nurture your plants throughout the season. And I apologize for revealing the harsh reality that you probably don't need to, generally shouldn't, and that **truly** unbridled kindness at the plant food trough will kill your big green buddies more surely than a sledgehammer.

Feel free to ignore my sage advice—go ahead and join my family! I know you're all against me! Sorry . . . But feed your plants every 2 weeks like a certain actor-turned-chemical-salesman tells you to on TV, and they'll look like you would if you ate a triple-size burger and fries three times a day.

But yes, I know you **have** to do **something.** And so. . . a safe way to feed your need without overfeeding your plants is to brew up some compost tea once a month or so during the season. It's fun, it can be really messy, your plants will love it, and *(perhaps most important)* it will provide you with something mysterious to do in public that your neighbors can point to and whisper guesses about and that you can later tell them is your secret for growing those beautiful tomatoes. *(Liar! It was the eggshells! But eggshells aren't romantic enough for you, are they? No, you need something sexier to be your "secret," something like . . . what? Oh. Sorry . . .)*

Simply place some nice, finished compost in a porous cloth container, sit it in a larger, much less porous container *(y'know, like a bucket)* filled with water, let it steep for 24 hours, and—voilà! You've got compost tea! You can make small, houseplant-size batches with an old sock and a half-gallon jug with the top cut off. Or fill up the pillowcase from that "dogs playing poker" sheet set, set it in a kitchen-size trash can full of water, and you'll make enough "tea" to feed a small garden. A burlap sack in a **big** trash can will satisfy a bigger garden.

When it's done steeping, remove the bag and return the contents to your compost pile. Thin the liquid with water until it's the color of tea *(if you* followed those precise measurements of mine correctly, the initial result should have been the color of coffee), and then just use it to water your plants. Wait until it hasn't rained for 4 or 5 days and then give each plant a little drinkie right down at the base—not too much right away, though! Give all your plants a first shot—about a pint or so—and then go around and do them all again, repeating the process until you're empty. (If you pour it all on at once, most of the tea will run off and give nearby weeds superpowers instead of feeding your tamatas.)

COMPOST ALTERNATIVES

WHY????!!! C'mon—you can't make it??? Don't know **anybody** who does??? Your township doesn't give it away??? Local nurseries don't sell it in bulk . . . .???

The truth is that compost **really** is #1, and it's a looonnnggg drive down to #2—which, by the way, is not the #2 you were thinking of if you were thinking of . . .

MANURE

Yes, I know the way your mind works. But be careful here. "Manure" has such a good image among gardeners that people don't think about its limitations, which include odor and handling issues as well as the risk of introducing dangerous pathogens into your garden. **Never put "raw" or "fresh" manure on your garden!**

If you have a handy source of "clean" manure (no dog or cat stuff; no factory-farmed-full-of-antibiotics material), and **if** you are willing to compost that manure until it loses all its most manurelike qualities, and **if** you then promise to **always** carefully wash your hands and everything you harvest from your garden before you take so much as a bite (my editor is a nervous Nellie here, and with all the animal disease, **E. coli,** and other outbreaks in the news—and that lawyer gnawing on her leg—I can't say I blame her. The lawyer's another story.), then it can be OK. But if you're not willing to do all that stuff, then skip the whole manure thing and use one of the many more desirable alternatives—like compost *(did I mention that compost's really good?)*. Oh, and even at its safest-handled best, manure's nitrogen-rich feedings often lead to big plants with few fruits. That's why I don't use any manure on my tamatas—not because of any health fears, but because I want tamatas, not fruit-free plants the size of Texas. **And** there's something better, safer, and easier to find . . .

GRASS CLIPPINGS

The real #2! Over the past couple of years, new research has emerged showing that grass clippings are a tremendously good source of nutrients—well-balanced ones, even! This is exciting *(and surprising)* news: A $1/2$-inch layer of grass clippings applied as a mulch around the base of your plants supplies all the food they'll need for a full season—and it's one of the absolute best mulches for keeping down weeds as well!

That's right—it's **not** compost, and yet I'm **not** knocking it! So go right ahead and use clips around your tomatoes if grass is abundant but compost is not. Probably better to lay a $1/4$-inch layer down early in the season and freshen it up 6 weeks or so later to avoid clumping and matting down; or add even smaller amounts more frequently.

JUST FEEDING THE TOMATOES!

Important note: Make sure your clippings come from a lawn that has **not** been treated with herbicides. Clippings from herbicide-treated lawns can kill garden plants when used as mulch. Not sure of your clippings' provenance? Don't take the risk.

WOOD CHIPS, SAWDUST, AND OTHER WOOD PRODUCTS

Don't use 'em unless you're willing to wait a couple of years to grow in that spot. Wood is the ultimate carbon source and will seek out nitrogen in an attempt to merge and decompose—and if you use it as mulch *(or—even worse—mix sawdust into your soil)*, it'll suck that nitrogen right out of your good earth **until it finishes decomposing.** And while it's bad to use too much nitrogen, all plants need **some.** Many is the gardener who accidentally starved his plants to death because he had a big pile of wood chips burning a hole in his trowel right around planting time, and "hey—they're natural, right?" Yes, they are. So is death.

PACKAGED FERTILIZERS

As long as it's organic *(hopefully it'll say "approved for use in organic agri-culture" or "certified organic" or "OMRI approved" somewhere on the package)*, it's likely to be okay.

Seaweed and kelp sprays or mixes can be very good as can mixtures of fish or fish meal and seaweed or kelp. Be wary of fish emulsion alone; these products are traditionally very high in nitrogen and some contain way too much chlorine. Avoid overly strong fertilizers and, like I keep saying, stuff that's too high in nitrogen *(represented by N—that first number on the fertilizer label)*. Like it says in "Solving the NPK Mystery!" on the opposite page, the ideal ratio of nutrients for fruiting plants like tomatoes is 3-1-2 *(or, as my friend Cheryl keeps calling it, "the NPK ratio that no dyslexic can ever remember correctly!")*.

It has its share of detractors these days, but **I like bonemeal.** It's a **great** source of phosphorus *(the P in NPK—the middle number on the bag o' fertilizer)*, which is **the** essential nutrient for getting lots of flowers and fruits. **And** bonemeal makes its phosphorus available faster than any other P source. *(That's not funny—stop laughing! This isn't Beavis and*

Butthead! Least not yet, it isn't. . . . And besides—**that** *"P" would be a source of* **nitrogen . . .)**

When I remember, I put a handful of bonemeal into each planting hole when I'm putting my transplants in. If I forget *(or can't remember* **if** *I remembered or forgot—what was I talking about?* **WHERE'S MY GINKGO???!!!***)*, I just dust a handful around each plant sometime later on. But you don't hafta if you don't wanna.

SOLVING THE NPK MYSTERY!

Actually it isn't much of a mystery—I'm just trying to get lots of keisters into the seats, like usual.

Take a look at any packaged fertilizer. Organic or chemical, powdered, granular, or liquid, it will have a set of three numbers displayed prominently on the label, like 10-10-10 *(bad)*, 5-3-5 *(better, but far from ideal)*, or 3-1-2 *(perfect, we now believe)*. Those numbers are that fertilizer's NPK ratio—the relative amounts of

> **Nitrogen (N),**
> **Phosphorus (P),** and
> **Potassium (K)**

that the fertilizer contains. Based on all the available evidence, it appears that a ratio of 3-1-2 is ideal for most garden plants. Turn the page for a little NPK101 *(hey!—that's my license plate number!)*.

Some folks worry that you might catch mad-cow disease from bonemeal 'cause it's made from cow bones. Others say that all the nutrition's been cooked away. And others fear that it will attract squirrels that will uproot the plants.

(Yawn.)

I use it and get lots of tomatoes.

Nitrogen (N): Like we've been saying, nitrogen is the basic plant food—it helps grow a big, strong "body" and lots of leaves. But feeding plants that you want to produce lots of flowers and/or fruits too much of this nutrient can limit the number of flowers and fruits because the plant is putting too much energy into making lush, leafy green growth instead of producing fruit. You will note that in our ideal 3-1-2 world, nitrogen is still the dominant nutrient. That's because nitrogen moves around so much in the soil that it needs to be replaced more often than the other nutrients. If your plants are slow to grow or show other signs of deficiency like yellow leaves *(which, unfortunately, is the symptom of just about every other tomato problem as well)*, go ahead and give them a nitrogen boost. Plants respond **very** quickly to nitrogen, so don't worry if you're playing catch-up—you **can** catch up with N. Good sources are grass clippings, alfalfa meal, bloodmeal, and fish products. Avoid recycled nitrogen from old liquid fuel ICBMs and Saturn booster rockets *(just seeing if you were still paying attention).*

Phosphorus (P): As far as I'm concerned, this is **the** key nutrient for top tomato production. It helps plants put down strong roots and encourages them to put out more flowers, which on tomatoes turn into well . . . tomatoes. So there. Because it **is** essential to strong root growth, you want this puppy to be in the soil right away. It's OK to add nitrogen later in the season, but you want your P to be there from day one. And it has to be right where the roots can reach it—phosphorus doesn't travel well in the soil like nitrogen does. That's why I toss that handful of bonemeal into each planting hole *(OK—**when** I remember; sheesh!).* Rock phosphate is another good source, but your soil has to be nice and acidic and alive for it to work its best; a product called colloidal rock phosphate is almost as P-rich but a **lot** less needy *(and it's especially good for use in sandy soils—it's a little "clayey" and it helps hold the sand particles together better).*

Potassium/potash (K): Why K? Because P was already taken! Why "potash"? I dunno—maybe it needed an alias. Anyway, it essentially helps plants do everything better. It helps the flow of all nutrients throughout the plant, improves fruit quality, and helps the plants better resist stress. Two good stand-alone potassium sources:

Greensand is a mined oceanic substance from the time of the dinosaurs that's found only in New Joisey. (Hey! That must be the secret behind the fabled Joisey tomato!!!)

■ **Greensand** contains only a small amount of potassium but has a big effect, perhaps due to all the neat little micronutrients it also provides. Greensand takes a while to break down, however—you really should add it to your soil the fall before you plant. Organic matter speeds its release, so some gardeners like to add greensand to their compost pile to supercharge the resulting "black gold"—a tactic I heartily recommend.

■ **Sul-Po-Mag** is organic, despite its Madison Avenue name, and is **very** powerful stuff. Also mined, but not in Joisey *(hey—nobody's perfect)*. A little goes a long way. Contains magnesium *(the "mag" part)* as well, so you wouldn't ever want to use more than a pinch on tomatoes—it could interfere with calcium absorption, which the plants need and love more. Hmmm. Come to think of it, much better to get this nutrient from greensand—or from compost or grass clippings; both are rich in K.

And that's just the tiniest little tip of the NPK iceberg. Maybe we'll do a *You Bet Your Fertilizers!* book and bore you some more later on.

SOIL TESTING

This is really fun to do, and most states offer a really inexpensive test through their County Extension Service—generally for under $10. You get in touch with your local extension office *(they tend to be listed in the blue pages of the phone book, under "County" or "Extension")*, and they send you a kit to put your sample in *(some nurseries sell the kits in spring as well)*. You fill it up *(make the sample*

nutrition in a nutshell

Now, there's just a few things I want you to be sure to take away from all this:

■ Compost really is the best—it supplies all the nutrients your plants need, in a form plants can use **easily.** Feed your plants with compost, and NPK can be just three more magnetic letters cluttering up the outside of your fridge.

■ If your plants are small, stunted, or otherwise don't seem to be growing, give them some nitrogen—alfalfa meal or bloodmeal or a fishy product *(emulsion or meal)*, but **don't** overdo it. And don't add these things if the plants are big and strong.

■ If you want to add some **really** helpful stuff to your soil, give each plant a handful of bonemeal and some greensand—although the greensand will work better if you add it to your compost pile and then feed the plants the finished compost.

■ If you buy fertilizer, make sure it's balanced. That **doesn't** mean equal numbers, like 5-5-5! The ideal is 3-1-2, so if you can't find that, shoot for 4-2-3 or something—try to stay in the same basic ratio. And don't let the numbers get too high *(which would also be an indication that the stuff ain't organic)*.

■ And don't overfeed! If you're using a packaged fertilizer, work the stuff into the soil when you put your plants in the ground, then mulch them with a thin layer of compost, and you should be set for the season. **Unless** you garden where it's **really** hot, and then you'll need to replace that compost more often.

a mixture of soil from all your big planting areas), send it in with a check, and you *(and often your local extension agent as well)* will receive the results. Most tests **don't** include your soil's nitrogen levels because they fluctuate a lot *(some tests **will** reveal your soil's "organic matter content," which is similar)*, but all will list the levels of phosphorus and potassium, the pH of your soil *(whether it's acid or alkaline—you want it to be a little on the acid side, like around 6.5 for most garden crops)*, and other cool stuff.

It's great to know what you have before you start adding things *(especially lime! Don't just go "liming your soil" because you saw some guy on TV do it! Get it tested first!)*, and it's fun— a horoscope for your dirt!

Last time I checked, the *OG* magazine Web site *(www.organic gardening.com)* had a wonderful list of soil test services for every state and Canadian province that included prices, available services, and contact info. *(**Note:** For some reason, soil tests for most West Coast states are either unavailable or darned expensive compared to the rest of the country; check the listings to see who will accept your out-of-state sample and you may save a good 50 bucks. Like there's a **bad** 50 bucks???)*

WATERING

Don't! Notice how I keep telling you **not** to do things? Most people do too many things. And watering often is often one of them.

Now this depends greatly on where you live. I garden in the land of traditionally wet summers, where plants rarely need extra watering. I did not water **once** last year, and the plants still got way too much from rain. And it is **really** difficult to remove water. **Much** easier to add, yessir.

But the previous year, I learned what it must be like to garden in Arizona. It rained not, and I learned that this can have a spiraling effect—the lack of rain literally sucked moisture out of the soil and made a theoretically correct amount of added water turn out to be much less than the plants actually needed. But I'm getting ahead of myself—let's start with the basics.

Bottom line: Keep track of your rainfall. *(An inexpensive rain gauge is a great investment.)* Here in the Northeast, we'll typically get one good soaking storm a week during the summer, and that's perfect. If a week goes by without one, it's time to water—but not 20 minutes a night every night for a week; that promotes shallow root growth, and your plants will go out and vote for whoever promises them a tax cut.

measuring **moistness**

Let's say you've lost track of all rainfall; you're an actor on one of those daytime soaps, and you've just emerged from a coma to find that your daughter has accidentally married your brother who misled a mob boss into thinking your car was gold-plated under that ratty yellow paint. **And** you don't know when it rained last. Stick your hand down into the soil a couple of inches. If you can feel moistness down there, back off. Don't water. If you can jam your finger down there to a depth of 6 inches or so *(and if you can, congratulations! You've got great soil! What's your secret, anyhow?)* and still feel only dry soil, go ahead and water.

Don't water just because the **surface** of the soil is dry! The top inch or so can dry out fast; it's how things are down by the root zone that counts.

And don't water just because the leaves of a plant are wilting and "it looks like it needs water." **Especially** if you've been pouring a bucketful on that poor baby every day for the past month, rain or shine. Because that's how **over**watered plants look, too.

"Oh no! My son fell overboard!"

"Here—I'll toss him my ice cubes!"

watering basics

An inch of water a week.

Really—that's it: what gardens, lawns, trees, those man-eating lily pads from the old "Tarzan" movies, and most other plants need "from you or the sky," as the saying goes.

You want to provide supplemental water like Nature does/did/should/isn't—a big, long soaker. I know, an inch of water doesn't sound like much, but think about those times it **poured** all night and then the local weather-guesser announced the next day on TV: "Boy, that was a soaker, wasn't it? We got three-quarters of an inch!" An inch is a lot. And since the best time to water is overnight, when the morning sun will dry the plants off quickly, I usually tell people to turn their sprinkler on when they go to bed and turn it off when they get up—unless they want to set the alarm for 5 A.M., turn the sprinkler off, take a leak *(never miss an opportunity, urged Winston Churchill)*, and go back to bed.

Anyway, give your garden a good soaking when you water, but only when you don't get that inch of natural rainfall.

If you're uncertain about how long it takes your particular sprinkler to deliver an inch of life-giving liquid, here's how to figure it out: Set a rain gauge, or cans, or milk cartons around the sprinkler area and then time how long it takes them to fill up to 1 inch. Then you can water for that length of time, using a timer if necessary. *(Just be sure to turn the timer off when rain delivers the water for you.)*

Don't give your garden *(or lawn, or whatever . . .)* a good soaking in the **evening** and then stop. It isn't good for **any** plant to sit around wet all night. A viable alternative *(and one I have used)* is to set that old alarm for 4 or 5 in the godforsaken, turn on the sprinkler, and then turn it off around 9 or 10 *(in the morning, of course)*. Obviously, if you have *(or get)* a timer for your sprinkler, you can do this without having to get up. But then you miss that chance for a free leak. Just thought I'd point that out.

And this really **is** what plants want. I know we **love** to water our landscape daily because it makes us look like good and decent people, but constant watering that never allows a plant's roots to dry out completely will literally drown the poor things. So you may look good and decent to others, but your plants will be dead.

And yes, plants really **do** want to have their tootsies dry out completely between waterings.

In a typical summer, with typical rain, you shouldn't be watering much, if at all—especially if you've got a nice mulch around the base of your plants to keep moisture in the soil. However, some gardens **will** dry out faster than others. **These include:**

- Gardens in full sun
- Gardens with unmulched plants
- Gardens with sandy soil
- Gardens in a blisteringly hot climate
- Gardens in any climate during a blisteringly hot, biblically dry season.

So use your head—pay attention to the conditions and be prepared to deviate from these suggestions if the weather goes all blahooey.

A COUPLE OF APPLICATION OPTIONS

Yes, it is much better to water at the base of your tomato plants than to use a sprinkler, which wets the leaves. *(Hey, so does rain.)* If you want to leave a hose dripping away at the base of each of your plants for an hour or so, and then move it to the next one, ad infinitum, fine. You can even do this any time of the day or night for all I care. And, yes, this could well be better for the plants than a sprinkler. But a sprinkler set up high in the middle of a garden sure can take care of everything at once. And you can run through it and get your shoes all muddy.

Drip irrigation uses little hoses that you *(typically)* bury in the soil that are connected to emitters that release small amounts of water over a long period of time to the root zone of plants; often controlled by a timer. They *(mostly)* water only where you want and thus water no weeds.

These systems *(or soaker hoses, below)* are probably well worth looking into if you live in a traditionally dry clime. I personally find them cumbersome and have never understood why people in **these** *(wet)* parts have them installed, but I have said previously that I don't judge, and I suppose I should try and keep that lie alive, respirator-bound as it is.

If you do use **true** drip *(root zone)* irrigation, feed your plants extra, as there are concerns about the water constantly washing nutrients away from the roots.

Soaker hoses are, to my little mind, a much better idea. Although they can be buried, most folks just lay them on top of the soil—maybe covered by a little mulch—around their plants. One type lets small amounts of water drip out through pinholes in the hoses *(what a great concept—pre-leaky hoses!)*. Another version "sweats" water out, soaking the nearby soil over time. They are much less tricky than in-ground drip irrigation systems, can be moved around easily to accommodate a changing garden plan and, if positioned correctly, water only the plants and not the pathways, thus greatly reducing weed growth.

Hmmm. Sounds pretty good, don't it? I actually used soaker hoses for many years and was quite happy with the results. But now I got a rotating sprinkler up on a big pole in the center of the garden. Does a great job of wetting everything down, I pull and toss the extra weeds into the compost, and we can shoo the kids out into it to wash the stink off 'em during the summer. You can't "go play in the soaker hose." Nope.

CHAPTER 6

Pest Control...

(Am I the only creature around here NOT
eating my tomatoes???)

...and CHAPTER 7

Dealing with Disease

(Can't we just take them to the hospital?)

Well now, you sad little gardener you, something has gone
terribly wrong out there, hasn't it? And it's driven you to
turn to this very special feature—two chapters in one—of
this very special book.

Oh c'mon—why **else** would you be reading these chapters??? There's no cutesy tomato names or fun tips about
grinding up the hubcaps of 1975 Chevy Novas and placing

a teaspoon of the resulting dust in each planting hole to supply the essential micronutrient molybdenum *(a deficiency of which, by the way, reveals itself in the form of yellow leaves on the plant. Unfortunately, as you are about to learn, so does just about every other nutrient deficiency,* **and** *three-quarters to 98 percent of the diseases that strike tomatoes.).*

Nope, you're here because you're in trouble. Or you've made an **incredibly** poor choice of reference material for a school paper.

Anyway, you've probably noticed that:

a) something other than you is eating your tamatas; or

b) your plants look like you did last flu season, stretched out on the couch in the middle of the afternoon, watching talk shows and doing shots of Nyquil every time someone says, "I just feel really self-empowered now."

The good news:

Pest problems on tomatoes are surprisingly rare and, when they do occur, are almost always pretty easy to deal with—organically, of course!

The other news:

Disease problems on tomatoes are about as rare as someone calling you up to ask if you're happy with your current long-distance provider.

Hey! Let's do those pests first then, shall we?

TOMATO PESTS

Probably the best known is the **tomato hornworm.** It's a big green caterpillar that feeds on the foliage of your plants *(almost never the fruits theyselves)* and is impossible to see 'cause it's the same color as the leaves it's eating. In fact, most people who **do** notice a hornworm actually

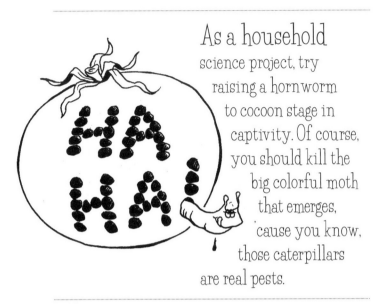

As a household science project, try raising a hornworm to cocoon stage in captivity. Of course, you should kill the big colorful moth that emerges, 'cause you know, those caterpillars are real pests.

first glimpse the neat-looking little white "spines" running down its back, which make it look a little like a stegosaurus, but much easier to squish.

If you see those white things, guess what? Pest problem solved!

Those "spines" are **not** standard equipment on your basic late-model hornworm. What looks a lot like little grains of white rice are actually the cocoons of a **TINY** *(wait a minute—then the letters should be small and not all caps!)* beneficial wasp that preys upon allkindsa pest caterpillars.

There are a lot of different species of such wasps flying around out there—some as small as the period at the end of a sentence *(you know, the part I rarely get to)*. All are too small to sting us, but they just **love** to lay their eggs in or on caterpillars. When the eggs hatch . . . that's right—just like in the movie *Alien*! But instead of Tom Skerrit, they're bursting out of **your** garden pests!

I **told** you organic gardening was fun!

If you see an **un**adorned *(buck-nekkid)* hornworm, just squish it. Or remove it from the plant, place it in a big container with a nonfruiting tomato branch in water, and try to keep it alive until it cocoons. If you see one with the white "rice" on its back, however, leave it be! *(OK—you can remove it from your tomatoes, but be sure to leave it in the garden.)* Soon, a fresh squadron of caterpillar-parasitizing mini-wasps will emerge from their cocoons to do garden pest control for you!

This, by the way, is Reason #162 for not using chemical pesticides in your garden. Today's pests mostly just shrug the poisons off *(thank you, Mr. Darwin!),* but when beneficial bugs get sprayed, they fold up faster than the Philadelphia Phillies making a run for the playoffs *(well, they* **could.** *Anything's* **possible,** *and hey, this book is supposed to make you laugh!).*

If I had written this book a year ago, I would not have included the **Colorado potato beetle** because *(OK now—everybody together)*: "It's a book about **t**omatoes, not **p**otatoes!" Thank you. That was nicely done.

But recently, a **huge** number of gardeners and garden writers and county extension agents and others living on the margins of decent society have told me of their tomato plants being eaten to the ground by these ravenous bugs. The larval *(baby)* form are kind of humpbacked, softish, and have round black spots on their side panels. The adults are less humped, have hard shell cases covering a set of wings *(as do all beetles, except Ringo, who worked by the hour),* and black stripes. Both stages are around $1/2$ inch long and orangish yellow and do a **lot** of damage—kind of like your cousin Earl, but smaller and without the pickup and the nasty dog.

I'm actually feeling a little sad and left out here. I mean, I've never had any potato bugs *(their generic, Mayberry-style* **nom de plume:** *"Opie! You been picking off them thar potato bugs for your Aunt Bee like you was supposed to, boy?")* on my tamatas. Now, my life has not exactly been pest- and problem-free, you know? But it's like I'm missing one baseball card out of a complete set . . . Garden Pests! Collect 'em! Trade 'em! Stick 'em in the spokes of your bike so they make noise! *(Ooouuuu—I* **like** *that one!)*

Your best CPB control option is a specific form of the organic insecticide *BT.* A number of different varieties of *BT (which stands for* Bacillus thuringiensis*)* are used in organic pest control—all are naturally occurring living organisms found in soils throughout the world. Lots of different strains of *BT* have been discovered, but only a few are being used, and all of those are used to kill pest insects. The mode of action is perfect:

You spray a solution of BT onto a plant and then, when the target pest nibbles away at the plant, the BT gets into the pest's stomach and shuts it down. So not only does the pest eventually die—it stops eating your stuff right away. The BT can't harm anything that doesn't eat it, and each variety of BT is so specific that it wouldn't even harm a different pest eating the same leaves. Needless to say, it won't harm you, your pets, your birds, your toads . . .

> If the dreaded CPB does come a calling on your German Johnsons, you really should do something about it. These thugs have decimated my potato plants in the past, so I know the damage they can do. And does.

BEETLES REUNION

REMEMBER WHEN WE PLAYED MIKE'S GARDEN? WHAT A PERFORMANCE!

The oldest and best-known form of BT (*variety* kurstaki, *or just* "BTK") is used to kill caterpillar pests. In fact, it's what you'd spray on your plants to control hornworms if those poor puppies weren't so pitifully vulnerable to teeny-tiny wasp attack already. For potato beetles, you want the variety *tenebrionis,* which is sold under the brand names Colorado Potato Beetle Beater *(nice and direct, eh?)* and Novodor *(which sounds more like the latest TV-advertised hair-loss treatment).* See "Cool-Stuff Sources" in da back of da book. *(Note: This BT's original variety name was* San Diego, *but apparently that was too easy to spell. So if you see a reference to* BT San Diego, *it's the same stuff.)*

Mix up a batch as directed and spray it on the leaves of your tomato plants *(do your potatoes, too).* The pests will die soon after eating the sprayed leaves.

Other control options: Hand-pick and drop the offenders into a jar of soapy water, or vacuum the suckers off! *(Works great—just be sure you're plugged into a ground-fault outlet or use a rechargeable vac.)*

76

If, like me, you must garden in a sometimes shady spot *(my garden is often shaded; the rest of the time it's pitch black)*, you'll probably have to deal with **slugs.** I hate slugs. *(I'd hate snails, too, but we don't have 'em here.)*

If you see big whopping holes in your fruits *(green or ripe)*, slugs have probably slimed their way up there and are dining on **your tomatoes** late in the evening while you sleep. The cowards. They must be killed. Daid. Twice. *(Have I told you yet how I feel about these scourges?)*

You can make sure it's slugs by going out into the garden—especially when it's still wet from a recent rain—late some evening *(after 10 P.M.)* with a flashlight, a spray bottle loaded with a 50-50 mixture of white vinegar and water, and a shaker filled with salt. If slugs **are** nibbling your plants, you'll see 'em. Spray some with the vinegar. See how they shrivel up! Look, Jane! Look at the slug! The slug is shriveling up, Jane!

You can also salt them. This is lots of fun. Don't salt them like French fries—just one little crystal on their slimy little selves is all it takes. You may not notice anything right away, but by morning, they'll be little blobs of orange goop. Don't do this too often 'cause you don't want to be salting your garden. Think of it as your occasional reward for staying up late.

Repulsed by the knowledge that this seething mass of living snot is out there devouring your precious garden plants every evening, you are now ready to wage war against these miserable mollusks. To wit:

■ Lay flat wooden boards down between your raised beds. The slugs, like vampires, will crawl under the boards when the sun rises. You go out early in the morning, lift the boards, and use a long, flat piece of metal or wood to scrape the massed slugs thereon into a bucket or something. Then do with your catch what you will. Have I mentioned yet what salt does to them? Just a thought . . .

Eventually you'll figure out that you're buying beer for creatures who are eating your garden to the ground. (And if you choose to continue anyway, two words: "cheap beer." Treat those slugs to the best case a 5-spot can buy.

■ You **CAN** leave out beer traps in which they will drown, but if you're thinking "Oh yeah—stale beer!" think again. Slugs like stale beer about as much as I do. Collect some old margarine tubs, fill them up with **fresh** beer *(the yeastier the better)*, and set them with the rims even with the soil surface around plants that have been attacked—at sunset, so the heat of the day doesn't flatten the brew. In the morning, they will be filled with drowned, drunken slugs. Empty your catch *(that nasty mess will now* **REPEL** *potential new victims)*, refill at sunset *(so the beer don't lose flavor during the day)*, and repeat.

■ Surround your plants with copper barriers; slugs can't touch copper *(it's like vampires and garlic)*.

■ Surround your plants with crushed-up eggshells; slugs can't slither over their pointy-sharp edges.

■ Buy a bag of diatomaceous earth and use it to make mystic circles around your plants. Looks like flour but is actually the pulverized remains of prehistoric ocean-dwelling creatures called diatoms. Very cool. Feels soft, but on a microscopic level is jagged and sharp and will pierce their mucousey little bodies. Wear a mask so you won't breathe the dust *(or* **any** *dusty garden stuff)*. You know how I worry.

Occasionally I hear from people whose tomatoes are being eaten by **squirrels**. I respond by saying, "Hey—do I tell you my troubles, pal???" They say, "Yes; in fact, I've read all your columns." Oh. Well, if it's any consolation, the squirrels aren't really interested in your tomatoes. They're either:

a) thirsty. In a dry season, squirrels will get water wherever they can, and your tomatoes are full of it. Leave some water out for them to drink, and just maybe they'll leave your love apples alone; or

b) amused. They love the performance you put on whenever they get near your tomatoes. Solution is easy: Move. To another state. Not an adjoining one, either. **Those** squirrels already heard about you.

Deer will also eat tomatoes. And everything else. If you don't have a garden, they'll eat your car. Good luck. *(Be sure to buy a copy of* You Bet Your Deer! *if I live that long.)*

Groundhogs will eat lots of your tomatoes. The surest way to keep them out is with a fence. But it *has* to be buried at least 1½ feet deep in the ground, preferably 2 feet *(they dig for a living)*, and you have to stake the regular straight-up part of the fence really well *(they can pull **real** hard)*, *and* you need *not* to stake the top foot, but to bend it outward, unsupported, like a baffle *(not like, actually—it **is** your baffle!)*. Yes, they climb. Really, really well. **But,** when they reach that outward-facing baffle, their

You come running out of the house, half-dressed and screaming and waving brooms and just being so darned amusing that they have to tell all the other squirrels for miles around about this great show.

fat and furry rear ends get plopped down on the ground—outside your garden. Fun to watch! 6-foot-tall fence: 2 feet buried, 3 feet staked, top 1 foot baffled out. Guaranteed.

Or get outdoor cats. Tough outdoor cats; no sissy-cat pretenders.

Or a Jack Russell terrier, of which there are no sissy-dog pretenders.

Birds. Also probably thirsty. Solution: Birdbath.

That's about it. Yeah, there's also things like tomato fruitworms and such *(the cure for which, by the way, is to spray BTK on your plants)*, but they're not all that common. More likely is your neighbors stopping by at the slug hour to filch some ripe ones. And that's **your** problem, honey chile.

TOMATO DISEASES

Like I warned you before, two wilts are very common tomato problems: **verticillium** and **fusarium.** These two fungal diseases are difficult to tell apart. Both begin with a yellowing and wilting of the lower leaves of your plant, which is real helpful, because yellow leaves are **also** a sign of:

- nitrogen deficiency
- iron deficiency
- zinc deficiency
- potassium deficiency
- calcium deficiency
- poor early childhood education
- aphids
- tobacco mosaic virus
- root-knot nematodes
- being too close to a black walnut tree
- the heartbreak of psoriasis

If you've fed your plants lots of nice compost *(or a good, balanced organic fertilizer)* and put some crushed-up eggshells into the planting hole like I told you to *(and you haven't recently spray-painted that nearby garage the center color on a stoplight)*, yellow leaves are probably not a sign of a hunger problem. Black walnut trees right nearby? You're outta luck. Buy a new house or plant in big containers next year.

If your tomatoes are planted where other tomatoes have grown in previous years, it could well be one of the wilts. Most likely verticillium, if you grow in a cooler clime *(like me)*, and fusarium for you warm-clime gardeners. Don't worry too much—unless they get really out of control, most plants will still provide you with tomatoes before they eventually succumb. Indeterminate plants—especially big, rangy heirlooms—can sometimes "outrun" the disease, with their aggressive new growth appearing faster than the old stuff can yellow up. Unfortunately, determinate plants don't run nearly as fast and will be knocked to the ground and have their lunch money taken away. In either case, the actual **tomatoes** are safe to eat.

But mark the areas where such plants are growing *(maybe you can buy a pack of little Skull and Crossbones pirate flags at the Dollar Store!)*, and don't put tomatoes in those spots again. **And** consider growing varieties known to resist these diseases next time out. Those tomatoes will have the letters V and F after their variety name on seed packets and in catalog descriptions. Most resistant varieties these days sport four letters—VFNT—meaning that they also resist those nematodes *(a serious problem down South)* and tobacco mosaic virus *(another reason not to smoke—you can make your tomatoes sick, too!)*.

Early blight is another fungal pest that'd just love to lay low your love apples *(and your potatoes, too)*. The first signs of this blight are targetlike spots on the lower leaves. These dark spots usually spread and run together. You might also see dark spots on the stems and *(shudder!)* on the stem ends of the bee-yoo-tee-ful tamatas themselves. This bad guy hangs out in debris in your garden, just waiting to infect next year's plants. So don't leave old tomato plants in the garden over winter.

There are a bazillion other diseases that can affect tomatoes—the further South *(and the more humid)* your growing location, the more diseases your patch will be prone to. *(But you'll also have a longer season than us cool climers and thus more of a replanting option when and if the Black Plague strikes—so don't complain. People in Syracuse only have—what?—about 18 frost-free days? Moan too loudly and we'll tell them where you live, and they'll use your garden as a snow dump next January.)*

Keep the compost coming—early blight is more likely to infect stressed plants (so maybe get out there and teach them some relaxation techniques before it's too late!).

And don't be surprised if one or two plants rot away on you while the others look fine, especially in a wet year. One plant coming down with the tomato flu does not necessarily mean it's going to spread through your garden like it was a day care center—especially if you do/have/does what follows:

As with us humans, it is easier to **prevent** tomato diseases than to cure them after they show up. So do the things I told you to do in the planting section, and you either won't have the problem to begin with or your troubles will be leetle ones. Specifically:

■ Keep the plants off the ground.

■ Make sure there's good air circulation around each plant.

■ Plant them where they get the earliest possible morning sun.

■ Keep $\frac{1}{2}$ to 1 inch of fresh compost on the soil around your plants.

- Don't plant tomatoes in that spot again for a few years.

- Light a candle to the blessed tomato deity of your choice.

If disease **does** show up:

- Remove any diseased leaves, stems, or even whole branches **immediately**. *(This slows down the spread of disease and confuses passersby into thinking your plants look great.)* Throw them in the trash. *(The diseased stuff, not the passersby.)* Do not compost or bury them. *(Be **especially** careful not to confuse plants with passersby in this case.)* If a whole plant looks **really** bad, pull it up and trash it. Really—it's Typhoid Mary in tomato drag.

- If you think "overreaction" is a term slackers coined to excuse their inherent laziness, you can remove all the old mulch from under and around the plant and replace it with $1/2$ to 1 inch of nice, fresh compost. This will eliminate any disease spores lurking on the ground, create a fresh layer of disease-munching microorganisms, and confuse the Jules Verne *(I got tired of saying "Dickens")* out of the slugs that were hiding there. *("Hey! Where'd Uncle Slimey go??!!")*

- If your plants are really crowded and some of the plants in that crowd are all yellowed up while others are fine, get the sad-looking ones outta there! Again, into the trash, **not** the compost!

- Do anything you can to improve airflow to the garden proper and especially to your languishing love apples. Yes, this may involve moving or simply removing another plant. Wet year? **Gotta** do it.

- Spray the secret formula(s) of your choice.

SECRET FORMULAS!

Of **course** it's a lie! Geez—hard to imagine you'd have gotten this far and not been able to smell when I'm selling tickets.

Anyway, although far from secret, these formulas **can** be very effective at preventing or fighting tomato disease difficulties.

Preventing: If you garden in a warm, wet clime, have had troubles with tomato disease in previous seasons, are forced to plant where tomatoes have gone before, or are just nervous as all get out about such things, you can use any of these formulas as a preventive. None of them will harm your plants, and the two compost tea ones will actually give 'em a nice little snack. You can spray these things as often as every 2 weeks—moving up to every week if the leaves of your plants begin to look a little suspicious.

Fighting: Get rid of all diseased leaves first. Spray the entire plant really really well, especially the undersides of the leaves—get in there and rub if you can, want to, and/or actually sort of enjoy feeling up your tomatoes. Then replace the mulch underneath (**not** *before you spray because you may wash undead disease spores down there).* Start out with weekly sprays, and then increase or decrease the frequency, depending on the response, the weather, and your patience for this sort of thing.

#1: Baking Soda and Oil—A Natural Plant Fungicide

Developed at Cornell University, this baking soda-based remedy is a great spray-on plant disease preventer/fighter. It's as good as any chemical fungicide you can buy. To use this formula, get a sprayer—anything from a handheld, 1-gallon job to one of those really cool big-boy backpack styles. Just make sure it's never been used to spray herbicides, or it's bye-bye Brandywines, baby!

In 1 gallon of water, mix:

1 tablespoon baking soda

1 tablespoon oil (see **Note** below)

1 or 2 drops dishwashing liquid

Shake well and then spray on the plant you wish to protect and/or rescue; keep shaking regularly while you're working. Shake the sprayer frequently as well.

Don't spray in direct sun in the heat of the day. Early morning is best; late evening is OK.

Note: The ideal "oil" to use here is "horticultural oil." Known to many folks generically as "dormant oil," that term actually refers to the old, original version, a very heavy petroleum-based product. For this recipe, you want to use one of the newer lightweight hort oils. Horticultural oil is available at most nurseries and garden centers. In a pinch, you can use regular vegetable oil from the kitchen, but a real hort oil will work better. And **no,** all you "duct-tape gardeners," you **can't** be a cowboy and use motor oil or WD-40 or any other such foolish thing. I will find out if you do and make you sorry.

#2: Basic Compost Tea

Many folks tell me that they've postponed, put off, and even successfully battled plant diseases by spraying regular old compost tea (CT) on their plants. And since it takes 2 weeks to make the superior-at-disease-fighting fermented version (described next), you might as well give it a try while your heavy artillery is brewing.

Make up a batch of CT like we told you to back on page 59. Strain the diluted "tea" through some cheesecloth (so it doesn't clog up your sprayer), then pour it into a sprayer tank, and spray on the plant's leaves the very first thing in the morning *(when the plants are most receptive to this kind of thing)*, making sure you get at the undersides of the leaves *(hold the sprayer low and shoot up)*. *Don't* spray in the heat of the day.

#3: Fermented Compost Tea

The killer. The winnah. Strongest plant disease fighter/preventer known to man (or wo-man). Tackles tomato diseases so hard it makes 'em cry. Defeats black spot on roses. Swear to God. This baby can't be beat.

To create fermented compost tea (FCT): Make compost tea. Pour an undiluted (strong coffee) batch into a big bucket and let it sit in a shady spot for 2 weeks. Cover the top of the container with window screening to keep out breeding mosquitoes, or you'll get a nasty surprise when you jiggle it the first time. Nasty scum will form on top of the liquid. This is good. Skim off scum and toss it back onto your compost pile. Yum. Then, *very* carefully and slowly, pour off some of the liquid that was underneath said scum through a fine strainer and into a sprayer. Slow down! There's a big batch of solids in the bottom of the bucket that you want to leave there, or you'll clog up your strainer. Toss these solids back into the compost pile, too.

Use FCT early in the season before the plants are fruiting, applying it as you would baking-soda-and-oil spray. Advantage of FCT over baking-soda-and-oil spray: The compost tea is *alive* with millions (maybe more) of tiny organisms that eat disease organisms. You're spraying Pac-Man–like soldiers that will literally eat diseases to death right there on your plants. Very exciting; just be sure to wash up thoroughly after you've applied FCT to make sure that you don't expose yourself to any errant bacteria. *(Yes, that lawyer has his teeth in my poor editor's leg again . . .)*

CHAPTER 8

The Harvest and Beyond

(Aren't they supposed to stop being green at some point?)

(So this one here cost me about 40 bucks, right?)

(Can the kids use the green ones to play Mr. Tomato Head?)*

Ah, there's nothing like seeing a big tomato plant loaded down with ripe red *(or black, or yellow, or orange, or purple, or . . .)* fruits sitting in the summer sun, is there?

NO, THERE ISN'T—BECAUSE IT'S STOOPID!!!!

. . . Unless you don't **like** experiencing the full, rich, complete, best possible taste of your tomatoes, that is.

*Answers: Sometimes, probably, and absolutely!

Revelation/Super Tip/Maybe you're not so sorry you bought this book after all: Tomatoes, especially the most flavorful heirloom varieties, are unique among the things we eat in that we experience much of their flavor through our nose. Really. Bite into a big pink *Brandywine,* and much of its great flavor is transmitted to your tomato-loving brain through your **olfactory** senses.

Much of a tomato's fine flavor is contained in volatile aromatic compounds produced in the ripening fruit. Read that again. See how the first word is "volatile," boys and girls? Can **you** say "volatile"?

HELPFUL HARVEST HINTS

I **like** the way you say that; yes, I do. Anyway, these are **volatile** aromatic compounds—so when you leave a ripe tomato sitting out in the sun, it loses flavor. Quickly. If you've always let your tomatoes get dead ripe on the vine before picking, you're in for a treat—start bringing them in more promptly and you'll note a tremendous surge in flavor. So:

Do not ever, under any circumstances, put a tomato in the refrigerator. You think heat dissipates those compounds? Well, cold'll finish 'em off. Don't do it. I'll know if you do, and I will find you.

1) Don't let ripe tomatoes sit on the vine; harvest them promptly.

2) Don't be shy about bringing them in early. Once it's started to color up, any tomato will finish ripening just fine on its own. I personally bring my tomatoes in once they're half colored up—at that point they're not getting nutrition or anything important from the vine; it's just support. Letting them finish ripening indoors gives me optimum flavor *and* protects the ripe and tempting fruits from last-minute pest *(slugs and deer love 'em!)* attack.

3) When you *do* bring your not-quite-fully-ripe ones indoors, **do not put them on the gosh-darned "sunny windowsill"!!!** That's what you just saved them from, fool!

GREEN TOMATOES

Green tomatoes are fun to eat!
Green tomatoes are really neat!
Hoooray! For green tomatoes!

Sorry. Anyway, at the end of the season you can either waste more hours of your life trying to protect your still-green tomatoes from frost by covering the plants with large sheets of plastic every night, **and then** removing those covers promptly every morning or your tomatoes will cook when the sun heats up that plastic like vinyl car seats in the summertime.

Or you can *(sound of angelic chorus rising majestically)*: **Be done!**

I say, be done and watch the World Series. Once **nighttime** temps stay consistently below 50°F, your tomatoes are pretty much in suspended animation anyway, and 20 years of experience has shown me that you expend around an 8-hour day's worth of work for every green tomato you actually coax a little more toward ripeness.

So when frost is called for, call the game as well. Strip all your green tomatoes off and bring 'em inside. If one or two plants are loaded with small fruits and you think it might **not** actually frost *(and you can smell the long, warm Indian summer that is* **certain** *to follow)*, sure, bundle those babies up in some nice, light floating row covers.

ALL of your green tomatoes that were getting ready to ripen or were at the "breaker stage" *(just beginning to show a blush of color)* will ripen up eventually if given long enough. And that's not a bad strategy. Just leave them out in the open—in a single layer, if at all possible—and use them as they ripen. Check them frequently—*especially* if they're piled up—for bad ones. A rotten tomato has an odor that repels skunks. That's why I sit my greenies out in long, low cardboard box bottoms that hold only one layer of 'maters *(no stacking!)*, and check 'em all every day.

Ripening on command. Well, pretty much on command. You can "push" a green tomato to ripeness by putting it *(or a bunch of its)* into a paper bag with a ripe banana, an apple, or a ripe tomato.

Those ripe fruits naturally give off ethylene gas, a manufactured version of which is used to gas-ripen commercial tomatoes, which are almost always picked green and hard for easy transport. This "natural gassing" will speed up the ripening process greatly. Roll the bag closed lightly—don't seal it shut or anything, and don't use plastic; a paper bag can "breathe." Make sure you check it *every* day, or . . . whoo! When'd you shower last?

Mr. Tomato Head. More greenies than you can possibly use? Give a couple of big hard ones to the kids, who can then play with Mr. Tomato Head from Outer Space! *('Cause he's green, see . . .)* Just:

1) Don't try this with ripe ones.

2) Save some to make fried green tomatoes.

3) Be sure to compost the body when playtime is done.

4) Remember—no pipe!

MY SUPER-FAST SAUCING TIP!

We grow most of our tomatoes to "put up"—like you have to do with me. Actually, this "putting up" involves sealing sauce and juice in Mason jars, which you may **also** want to do with me at this point.

Anyway, to get a really rich flavor, we sauce together lots of different kinds of tomatoes, mostly big heirlooms like *Georgia Streak, Brandywine, Mortgage Lifter,* and *Black Krim,* along with traditional pasters like *Roma* and *Bellstar,* and less-traditional ones like *Amish Paste* and such.

Those big, juicy ones add lots of flavor to the finished product but make it harder to get there because they *also* add lots of nonmeaty liquid to the mix. Over the years, we've developed a method that gives us lots of nice, thick sauce **quickly**—which is not only important in time saved, it also helps preserve the vitamins in the finished stuff. Here's the technique, along with my basic sauce-making recipe, so you can continue to enjoy that harvest—maybe even up until you got some fresh ones again!

1. Collect all your nice, ripe tomatoes, wash them well, and cut them right down the center so you can easily carve out the stem part. If a tomato has a few imperfections or bug holes, cut them away completely as well. If in doubt about a tomato's wholesomeness, don't use it.

2. Other people remove the skins; I don't—it's nice solid tomato stuff and contains nutrients not found in other parts. And the Vita-Mix food processor I use is so powerful they just disappear into the blend.

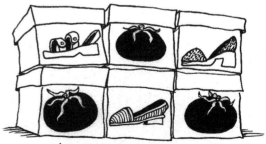

MRS. McGRATH'S FALL CLOSET

3. Chop your tomatoes up in batches and mostly fill up a blender or food processor with each chopped batch. Before whizzing, add one or more of the following to each batch:

Onions: I add two or three big ones to each pot of sauce
Garlic: I add three or four *bulbs*—not cloves, *bulbs*—to each pot.
Herbs: Basil, oregano, whatever you like, whatever you got.

4. Chop your seasoning things up finely and whiz each up well with your current batch of actual tomatoes *(this mixes the seasonings in better than you could possibly achieve otherwise)* and pour the resulting glop into a big stainless steel *(not aluminum!!!)* stockpot. Simmer on low once you got a couple inches of stuff in the pot.

5. When everything's all in the pot, give it about 20 minutes to heat up. *(In the meantime, get your canning stuff together: glass jars that have just been washed and are still nice and hot from the dishwasher, a pot of water to heat your lids, a big pot of water heating up to do the actual canning in, etc.)* Add a dash or seven of soy sauce and some ground black pepper to the pot, and stir well. *(Some people would sweeten their sauce at this point. Don't be like them.)*

6. Now the cool part. You'll notice that the really liquid stuff is all rising to the top. Get another stainless steel pot and a strainer. Using a big-handled cup, keep skimming the liquid stuff off the top and pouring it through the strainer into that other pot. Anything that gets stuck in the strainer goes back into the sauce pot. Keep going, stirring the now-rapidly thickening sauce as you do. When the liquid is mostly gone, begin using the stuff that gets trapped in the strainer to fill your first run of jars—a nice batch of wonderfully thick sauce.

7. You can simply jar the liquid stuff up separately when you have all the sauce done, or you can add another level of coolness. That liquid will also separate, with a light tomato juice rising to the surface and lots of pastey-type solids dropping to the bottom. If you have a big, sparkling-clean glass jar, pour your "juice" into it and wait 5 minutes—you'll see a clear line of demarcation. Using a clean turkey baster, suck the lighter-colored thin stuff off the top. I put this in quart-size glass jars in the fridge and use it to make tomato soup or in place of some of the cooking water when I make soup stock.

8. Can up the darker-colored stuff that settles down low. You can use this "almost tomato paste" to make ridiculously rich tomato soups or, with a little cooking down, a wonderful, naturally smooth sauce.

9. Follow the canning directions that came with your canning jars and lids *exactly*. Tomatoes are the easiest foods to can—their high acid content makes them one of the only foods you can "put up" safely without a pressure cooker. But still, be careful—make sure the jars are **REALLY** sterilized *(I always time a dishwasher run so the jars are clean and hot when the sauce is ready)*, that everything you use is good and clean, wipe the tops of the jars with a clean, dry paper towel before you put the lids on, and all that stuff. I generally cook my pints of sauce, juice, and paste for 20 to 30 minutes in the canner.

10. Enjoy, brag, be proud!

That's it! Thanks, have fun, and I'll see you next book. *(Oh, sure, that's what's you say* **NOW!** *But you're hurt, you're angry. The pain will fade away.)*

I know you—you'll be back.

Mike McGrath

Mike McG

93

COOL-STUFF SOURCES

Should your locale be lacking in a suitably well-stocked garden center, here are some mail-order suppliers who can help you on your way to homegrown tomato nirvana.

SEEDS

Bountiful Gardens
18001 Shafer Ranch Road
Willits, CA 95490
Phone: (707) 459-6410
Fax: (707) 459-1925
Web site:
www.bountifulgardens.org

W. Atlee Burpee
300 Park Avenue
Warminster, PA 18974
Phone: (800) 888-1447
Fax: (215) 674-4170
Web site: www.burpee.com

The Cook's Garden
P.O. Box 535
Londonderry, VT 05148
Phone: (800) 457-9703
Fax: (800) 457-9705
Web site: www.cooksgarden.com

Fedco Seeds
P.O. Box 250
Waterville, ME 04903
Phone: (207) 873-7333
Fax: (207) 872-8317

Garden City Seeds
778 Highway 93 North, #3
Hamilton, MT 59840
Phone: (406) 961-4837
Fax: (406) 961-4877
Web site:
www.gardencityseeds.com

Heirloom Seed Project
Landis Valley Museum
2451 Kissel Hill Road
Lancaster, PA 17601
Phone: (717) 569-0401
Fax: (717) 560-2147

Johnny's Selected Seeds
1 Foss Hill Road
R.R.1 Box 2580
Albion, ME 04910
Phone: (207) 437-4301
Fax: (207) 437-2165
Web site: www.johnnyseeds.com

Nichols Garden Nursery
1190 Old Salem Road NE
Albany, OR 97321
Phone: (541) 928-9280
Fax: (800) 231-5306
Web site: www.nicholsgarden
  nursery.com

Park Seed Co.
1 Parkton Avenue
Greenwood, SC 29647
Phone: (800) 845-3369
Fax: (864) 941-4206

Web site: www.parkseed.com
Pinetree Garden Seeds
P.O. Box 300
New Gloucester, ME 04260
Phone: (207) 926-3400
Fax: (888) 527-3337
Web site: www.superseeds.com

Seeds of Change
P.O. Box 15700
Santa Fe, NM 87506
Phone: (888) 762-7333
Web site: www.seedsofchange.com

**Southern Exposure
Seed Exchange**
P.O. Box 460
Mineral, VA 23117
Phone: (540) 894-9480
Fax: (804) 894-9481
Web site:
www.southernexposure.com

Stokes Seed Inc.
Box 548
Buffalo, NY 14240
Phone: (716) 695-6980
Fax: (888) 834-3334
Web site: www.stokeseeds.com

Territorial Seed Company
P.O. Box 158
Cottage Grove, OR 97424
Phone: (541) 942-9547
Fax: (888) 657-3131
Web site: www.territorial-seed.com

Tomato Growers Supply Co.
P.O. Box 2237
Fort Myers, FL 33902
Phone: (888) 478-7333
Fax: (888) 768-3476
Web site: www.tomatogrowers.com

Totally Tomatoes
P.O. Box 1626
Augusta, GA 30903
Phone: (803) 663-0016
Fax: (888) 477-7333
Web site: www.totallytomato.com

GARDENING SUPPLIES/SOIL TESTING

Arbico
18701 North Lago Del Oro Parkway
Tucson, AZ 85739
Phone: (800) 827-2847
Web site: www.goodearthmarket
   place.com

Gardener's Supply Co.
128 Intervale Road
Burlington, VT 05401
Phone: (888) 833-1412
Fax: (800) 551-6712
Web site: www.gardeners.com

Gardens Alive!
5100 Schenley Place
Lawrenceburg, IN 47025
Phone: (812) 537-8650
Fax: (812) 537-5108
Web site: www.gardensalive.com

Green Spot Ltd.
93 Priest Road
Nottingham, NH 03290
Phone: (603) 942-8925
Fax: (603) 942-8932
Web site: www.greenmethods.com

Harmony Farm Supply
3244 Highway 116 North
Sebastopol, CA 95742
Phone: (707) 823-9125
Fax: (707) 823-1734
Web site: www.harmonyfarm.com

Peaceful Valley Farm Supply
P.O. Box 2209
Grass Valley, CA 95945
Phone: (530) 272-4769
Fax: (530) 272-4794
Web site: www.groworganic.com

Snow Pond Farm Supply
P.O. Box 70
Salem, MA 01970
Phone: (978) 745-0716
Fax: (978) 745-0905
Web site: www.snow-pond.com

Woods End Research Laboratory
P.O. Box 297
Mt. Vernon, ME 04352
Phone: (800) 451-0337
Fax: (207) 293-2488
Web site: www.solvita.com

ACKNOWLEDGMENTS

Thanks to all who worked on this book, especially my friends Deb Martin, Diana Erney, and the wonderful Signe Wilkinson—the toughest, funniest Quaker broad I know.

INDEX

Note: Of course everything is indexed under Tomatoes! Where else would you look for information in a book about tomatoes? By the way, page numbers in **boldface** indicate tables.